T0295812

Starbucks

Starbucks

Second Edition

Marie A. Bussing

Corporations That Changed the World

An Imprint of ABC-CLIO, LLC
Santa Barbara, California • Denver, Colorado

Library of Congress Cataloging-in-Publication Data

Names: Bussing-Burks, Marie, 1958– author.
Title: Starbucks / Marie A. Bussing.
Description: 2nd edition. | Santa Barbara, California : Greenwood, [2022] | Series: Corporations that changed the world | Includes bibliographical references and index.
Identifiers: LCCN 2021012162 (print) | LCCN 2021012163 (ebook) | ISBN 9781440873881 (hardcover ; alk. paper) | ISBN 9781440873898 (ebook)
Subjects: LCSH: Starbucks Coffee Company. | Coffee industry—United States.
Classification: LCC HD9199.U54 S732 2022 (print) | LCC HD9199.U54 (ebook) | DDC 338.7/6164795—dc23
LC record available at https://lccn.loc.gov/2021012162
LC ebook record available at https://lccn.loc.gov/2021012163

ISBN: 978-1-4408-7388-1 (print)
      978-1-4408-7389-8 (ebook)

25 24 23 22 21   1 2 3 4 5

This book is also available as an eBook.

Greenwood
An Imprint of ABC-CLIO, LLC

ABC-CLIO, LLC
147 Castilian Drive
Santa Barbara, California 93117
www.abc-clio.com

This book is also available on the World Wide Web as an eBook.

Visit www.abc-clio.com for details.

ABC-CLIO, LLC
130 Cremona Drive, P.O. Box 1911
Santa Barbara, California 93116–1911

This book is printed on acid-free paper

Manufactured in the United States of America

Although the author has made every effort to ensure the accuracy and completeness of information contained in this book, we assume no responsibility for errors, inaccuracies, omissions, or any inconsistency herein. Any slights of people, places, or organizations are unintentional.

The following are trademarks of Starbucks Corporation or other organizations:

Black Apron Exclusive	Pike Place Roast
Caffè Verona	Seattle's Best Coffee
Clover Brewing System	Starbucks
Ethos	Starbucks Doubleshot
Fair Trade Certified	Starbucks Duetto
Frappuccino	Starbucks VIA
Gold Coast Blend	Vivanno
Natural Decaf	

Starbucks Corporation owns numerous trademarks, with the following trademarks being of material importance:

Starbucks	Seattle's Best Coffee
The Starbucks logo	Teavana
Starbucks Reserve	Frappuccino

Dedicated to my daughters,

Amie and Katie

Contents

Acknowledgments

I would like to thank Maxine Taylor, Senior Acquisitions Editor, Health/ Wellness and Psychology, at ABC-CLIO, for allowing me this exciting opportunity to explore the transitioning business practices of Starbucks. So much has changed since I wrote the first edition over ten years ago— digital innovation, food delivery services, strawless lids, and exploration in new countries. It has been an interesting learning experience uncovering how the coffee company has recognized challenges and created opportunities.

My sincere gratitude is also extended to Cathy Bowman for her outstanding editorial assistance. It is greatly appreciated and valued.

A group of highly skilled professionals in the fields of coffee, philanthropy, and business shared their time and expertise in the development of this book. I owe a debt of gratitude to Chris Manfredi, president of the Hawaii Coffee Association; Vicki Rubio, program director at Public Allies; Anne-Marie Taylor, executive director at Indianapolis Neighborhood Resource Center; Ted Lingle, executive director for Coffee Quality Institute; and a spokesperson from the ICE Futures U.S. The input from these experts highlighted details on finance, community, and the coffee industry. Their wide-ranging knowledge added significantly to the depth of this text.

Finally, thank you to Jim for his endless support and encouragement.

Introduction

Is not the very name, COFFEE, suggestive of aromatic odors?
—Robert Hewitt Jr., *Coffee: Its History, Cultivation, and Uses* (1872)

Java, cup of joe, bean juice, mocha, or just plain coffee—whatever you call it, this beverage conjures up feelings of comfort, warmth, and kinship. A morning eye-opening ritual for many, pots of this black beverage brew in homes, offices, restaurants, and, of course, coffeehouses, throughout the day. As the world's largest consumers, Americans drink approximately 400 million cups of coffee each day.

Did You Know?

Coffee is the world's second most traded commodity. Do you know the first?
    You guessed it—oil.

How did this steaming roasted bean come to permeate our lives and our culture? The story of coffee dates back more than one thousand years. It has swept the globe, only to explode in Seattle, Washington, now the symbolic Coffee Capital of the World. The coffee tree is native to Ethiopia. In fact, the name *coffee* is thought to be a derivation of Kaffa, an Ethiopian province.

A popular legend maintains that the origin of coffee can be traced to a simple Ethiopian goat herder named Kaldi. One day while tending the flock, Kaldi observed his goats dancing. They had been eating bright red coffee berries and, out of curiosity, Kaldi chewed a few himself. He discovered the invigorating effects of the beans and soon began dancing with his goats.

Kaldi shared the story of the special berries with a monk from a nearby monastery. The monk threw the berries onto an open fire, suspecting evil. A wonderful aroma filled the air and the holy man changed his mind, scooping the beans from the fire to make a watery beverage with the powder. Hence, the first cup of coffee. The monk and his fellows drank the substance in order to stay awake during their all-night religious ceremonies.

It is known that East African tribes would mix ground coffee beans into a paste with animal fat. This mixture provided energy to their warriors and was a primitive version of today's power bars.

Coffee was taken from Ethiopia to the Yemen province of Arabia in the 15th century. Serious cultivation of the trees began at that time by the Yemenis, long famous as the world's suppliers of coffee. The Arabs guarded their monopoly on coffee and made exportation of coffee plants illegal so the crop could not be grown elsewhere. Before coffee beans could be sold, they were boiled to make them infertile. The coffee bean trade was first centered in the Yemeni port of Mocha and then expanded to Mecca, the most important trading center of the world, to Turkey, and to Egypt. Coffee's popularity became widespread throughout the Islamic world. In fact, the first coffeehouses were opened in Mecca and called kaveh kanes, a religious gathering location that transformed into social gathering place where coffee was consumed. It was against the Muslim faith to drink wine or other alcoholic spirits, so coffee became a favored alternative. Coffeehouses quickly spread throughout the Middle East during the 15th century as places where men would gather to drink coffee, sing, tell stories, listen to music, and play chess. Although banned in subsequent periods of history for their role in political controversy, coffeehouses were an integral part of Islamic culture during this time.

The Dutch were the first to carry a live coffee seedling out of Yemen, transporting it to Holland in 1616. There, the seedlings were grown in greenhouses. The Dutch began cultivating large-scale plantations in their colonies in Indonesia, on the islands of Java, Sumatra, Sulawesi, and Bali. Soon, the Dutch colonies were the main suppliers of coffee for all of Europe. Coffee was widespread in Europe by the mid-17th century, especially in England, France, and Holland.

In 1720, a French naval officer named Gabriel Mathieu de Clieu, serving on the Caribbean island of Martinique, acquired a coffee seedling while in Paris on leave. His goal was to get the tree back to Martinique safely, but a threat from pirates, a terrible storm, and even a jealous fight over the coffee plant all marked the ship's journey. When drinking water was rationed, de Clieu unselfishly gave up most of his water ration to keep the coffee plant alive. The plant miraculously survived the trip and thrived in its new environment. By 1777, it is recorded that there were between 18 million and 19 million coffee trees on Martinique.

Meanwhile, coffeehouses were gaining popularity all over Europe as centers of social interaction where people could talk, read, or write in solitude. The first coffeehouse opened in Britain in 1652. The British called their coffeehouses Penny Universities because that was the price for admittance to the shop where one could drink coffee, read newspapers, and do business. Information exchanged at the coffeehouse was invaluable for businessmen conducting transactions. Business was handled very informally at the time. Notably, in 1686, Edward Lloyd opened a coffee shop that became a center for marine insurance. Lloyd welcomed those interested in overseas trade, such as ships' captains, merchants, and ship owners. Merchants with ships would ask a broker to find wealthy individuals to risk their personal fortunes on the ships and cargo. That coffeehouse eventually evolved into the world-renowned Lloyd's of London insurance company, today home to the most experienced specialist underwriters in the world. In England, as in America, the purpose of the early coffeehouse was business.

The first mention of drinking coffee in North America dates from 1668, and coffeehouses soon followed. The Tontine Coffee House in New York was the original location for the New York Stock Exchange in 1792 because regular business and transactions were conducted there. In the United States, the coffeehouse cultural scene bloomed in the early 1960s. Writers, musicians, and intellectuals used coffeehouses as venues for their work, often accompanied by guitarists, folk musicians, and poets freely expressing their thoughts and political leanings in an open atmosphere. The coffeehouse scene thrived in the Pacific Northwest, and Starbucks was soon at the forefront.

On March 29, 1971, Starbucks opened its first store in Seattle, in the Harbor Heights Hotel at Pike Place Market. Starbucks might have begun as one local roaster and retailer, but today it has transitioned into the largest coffeehouse chain in the world with more than 32,000 locations in eighty-three countries. The stores carry a variety of handcrafted beverages, coffee drinks, teas, food items, roasted beans, and coffee accessories.

In five decades, Starbucks has earned phenomenal success. It has changed the way people enjoy coffee, so much so that the Starbucks experience is an important part of people's lives, with 100 million customer experiences occurring each week. Despite challenges along the way, this success story had a game plan. Let's explore the story of Starbucks, its strategy, and how it became a corporation that changed the world.

Did You Know?

Coffee is produced in over seventy countries and provides a living for 25 million coffee farmers around the world.

CHAPTER ONE

Origins and History of Starbucks

Starbucks didn't invent coffee, of course; it just did something with it that no one thought possible.
—Taylor Clark, *Starbucked: A Double Tall Tale of Caffeine, Commerce, and Culture* (2007)

Before Starbucks, going out for coffee meant a cup of steaming black brew, friendly conversation, and sharing the booths with neighboring breakfast and lunch customers. But in just a few decades, Starbucks would completely change the American coffee scene. High-priced brews, lattes, Frappuccinos, and espressos awaken the senses for 100 million customers every week around the world. Touting more than thirty blends and single-origin coffees, Starbucks has more than 170,000 customizable drink combinations when you consider the fine details of milk add-ins, shots, syrups, and whips.

Three Seattle friends started the company—Gordon Bowker, Jerry Baldwin, and Zev Siegl. Bowker was a writer, Baldwin was an English teacher, and Siegl was a history teacher. The original name of the first store, opened in 1971, was Starbucks Coffee, Tea, and Spices. Later, the name was changed to Starbucks Coffee Company. Starbucks' original logo was a chocolate brown, bare-breasted mermaid siren with long hair, encircled by the company name. The fourth and current logo, redesigned in 2011 to celebrate the fortieth anniversary of the company, still sports the mermaid but with a more updated green design and absent of words.

Starbucks was named after Starbuck, first mate of the whaleship *Pequod* in Herman Melville's *Moby Dick*. Terry Heckler, with whom Bowker had an ad agency, had looked at an old mining map of the Cascades and

Mount Rainer one day, spotting a town called Starbo. The name Starbo reminded Bowker of the first mate in *Moby Dick*, Starbuck. The character had nothing to do with coffee; Bowker just liked how the sound of the word "popped." Starbuck was pluralized for ease of use and was approved by the trio.

The friends were not skilled in the coffee business. At the time, all they knew was that a good cup of coffee was hard to find. One day over lunch, Bowker was discussing the beans he had purchased on one of his monthly trips to Vancouver, British Columbia, to purchase coffee. That was the nearest place he could get a decent cup of coffee. They all preferred coffee from dark-roasted arabica beans, rather than the lower-quality, less-flavorful robusta beans more commonly used. Tired of importing his own beans on his monthly runs to Canada, Bowker and his two friends dreamed up the scheme of selling coffee in Seattle, and Starbucks was born.

The Beginnings

Bowker, Baldwin, and Siegl knew they needed the right coffee to sell. Siegl went south to California to find the goods. A Dutchman, Alfred Peet, was doing big business from his storefront in Berkeley—Peet's Coffee & Tea. Siegl knocked on his door looking for someone to roast coffee for Starbucks. Peet agreed to supply the fledgling shop with coffee if the founders would each work at his Berkeley shop for a week to train in the coffee business. So, for Starbucks' first year in business, Peet roasted the beans while teaching his entrepreneurial friends. Bowker, Baldwin, and Siegl visited Peet's many times to learn about quality coffee and proper roasting techniques from this master.

According to Taylor Clark, the three invested $1,350 each and together borrowed $5,000 from the bank. Rent on the first store was just $137 a month (*Starbucked: A Double Tall Tale of Caffeine, Commerce and Culture*, 2007, 41–42). Overhead costs were low. Initially, Starbucks did not even sell fresh-brewed coffee by the cup, though samples were available for drinking from porcelain cups. The original purpose of the store was to sell gourmet coffee beans, along with coffee-related merchandise and equipment.

At the start, Siegl was the only paid employee at Starbucks. He wore an apron, scooped the coffee beans, connected with his customers, and was the retail guru. During the first year, Starbucks ordered its coffee beans from Peet's. But when the Seattle shop started moving significant amounts of coffee, Peet could not keep up with the demand and the partners had to come up with a new plan. They purchased a used coffee roaster from

Holland, set up roasting operations, and began experimenting with blends and flavors on their own. Bowker and Baldwin tinkered with Peet's roasting procedures, creating their own unique blends. Baldwin became an accomplished roaster, and Bowker was the marketing genius.

The fact that Starbucks was born and survived the early 1970s in Seattle is a feat in and of itself. Boeing, a major aerospace and defense corporation, was then headquartered there. (In 2001, Boeing moved its headquarters to Chicago, but production remains in Seattle.) Boeing, the city's largest employer, went into a major economic downturn just as Starbucks was getting started, due to a national aviation recession. That was topped off by Congress withdrawing funding for the production of an American supersonic transport Boeing had developed. The company cut its workforce from 80,400 in early 1970 to 37,200 by October 1971. Many people, unable to find work in the area, were forced to move away. The situation was so extreme that two real estate agents, with a hint of humor, put up a billboard on the city's outskirts that read "Will the last person leaving Seattle—turn out the lights?" However, Seattle did recover after the Boeing crash, and Starbucks coffee sales helped stimulate the local economic recovery.

The first Starbucks store was located in a storefront at the Harbor Heights Hotel at Pike Place Market, where it remained from 1971 to 1976. The flagship store then moved to 1912 Pike Place in Pike Place Market, where it remains today. It was a rustic store, small, with a nautical theme. With the entrepreneurial talents of Baldwin, Bowker, and Siegl, Starbucks slowly grew. A second store opened in the city in 1972. Ten years later, in 1981, Starbucks had a roasting plant and four Seattle retail stores selling whole-bean coffee. Although the company was profitable, in 1980, Siegl decided he wanted to leave Starbucks and pursue other interests. He sold out that year. He felt Starbucks had grown too large, and he was more effective in smaller businesses. The roles of the remaining duo shifted, as Baldwin served as president and took over daily operations. Bowker, although still involved with Starbucks, also had outside interests—writing and other entrepreneurial adventures.

Did You Know?

If you visit 1912 Pike Place, don't expect the modern updates of your favorite Starbucks location. Everything is original, including the flooring, fixtures, and the bar. In the window, you will even see the original siren sign touting the Starbucks Coffee, Tea, and Spices logo.

The New Player

One of the items found on Starbucks' shelves was the Hammarplast coffeemaker. Hammarplast sold Swedish-designed kitchen equipment and housewares. In 1981, an executive at Hammarplast became curious about why a small retailer in Seattle was ordering large quantities of the company's thermos-type drip coffeemakers. Upon traveling to the Starbucks flagship store in Pike Place Market, Howard Schultz discovered the shop that sold only whole-bean coffee and coffee merchandise and equipment—including Hammarplast coffeemakers in red, yellow, and black. He was instantly intrigued and enamored with the promise he saw in this small retailer. During the next year, the New York-based housewares executive applied and was hired as Starbucks director of retail operations and marketing. Schultz took a steep pay cut, but in addition to his salary he was given a small equity share in the business—a share of the company's future. The destiny of Starbucks was changed forever.

In the spring of 1983, Schultz attended an international housewares show in Milan. He was impressed with the Milan espresso bars and the whole Italian coffee bar culture, offering community, camaraderie, and artfully prepared coffee. Starbucks was selling great coffee beans, but it did not serve coffee. Samples were served only in order to give customers a chance to taste the product before buying beans by the pound. Serving coffee and espresso the Italian way, Schultz imagined, could change Starbucks from a great retailer into *an experience*. He returned to Seattle with a new vision.

When Starbucks opened its sixth store in April 1984, the founders allowed Schultz to test his coffeehouse concept. That store, at the corner of Fourth Avenue and Spring Street in downtown Seattle, was the first Starbucks designed to sell coffee by the pound alongside prepared coffee beverages—regular cups of brewed coffee as well as the then-unfamiliar espresso drinks so popular in Europe. The response was overwhelming. While a high-performing Starbucks had previously tallied an average daily customer count of 250, within two months, the new store was serving 800 customers per day. The beverage business was definitely a success. But the founders chose not to take the idea of espresso bars any further, deciding rather to concentrate on the business of coffee roasting.

Starbucks, which was majority owned by Bowker and Baldwin, bought out Peet's Coffee & Tea in 1984. The founders were preoccupied with the acquisition and merging of the two companies and were not supportive of the espresso business. Schultz, on the other hand, wanted to open additional stores that would serve coffee and espresso, intent on capturing the warm social interaction he had experienced and admired in Italy.

Convinced the espresso bar concept would be a hit with Americans, Schultz left Starbucks and began his own coffeehouse business. Schultz started the Il Giornale coffee bar chain in 1985. *Il Giornale* is the name of Italy's largest newspaper. *Giornale* means daily; if the company served great coffee, Schultz hoped customers would come back every day. The coffeehouse sold brewed coffee and espresso beverages. About thirty investors, including Starbucks, which pumped in $150,000, contributed $1.65 million to back the new venture. All beverages were made from Starbucks coffee beans.

On April 6, 1986, the first Italian-style Il Giornale coffeehouse opened. It was a tiny, 700-square-foot store near the main entrance to Seattle's tallest building. Within six months of opening, it was serving 1,000 customers a day.

Did You Know?

Coffee trees grow roughly 40 feet high. Coffee plants produce cherry-like fruits which contain two seed halves, called coffee beans. It is in the pit of the fruit that you will find the green, unroasted coffee bean.

Change on the Horizon

Bowker and Baldwin eventually became disenchanted with the business development of their start-up. Baldwin wanted to concentrate on the core business of selling quality coffee beans and focused his interests on the Peet's acquisition. Bowker was busy with a variety of business ventures. Wanting to do other things, he was pleased to take some cash out of the business. In 1987, Baldwin and Bowker sold the Seattle stores, the roasting plant, and the name Starbucks—keeping only the Peet's assets. In a nearly $4 million deal backed by local investors, Il Giornale acquired the Starbucks assets and changed the unified company's name to Starbucks Corporation. Starbucks was thought to be a catchier and easier-to-pronounce name for Americans than the Italian Il Giornale. Expansion began immediately, aiming toward Schultz's goal to build an international company. Starbucks opened its first locations outside of Seattle in Chicago and Vancouver, British Columbia. By the end of the first fiscal year, Starbucks had seventeen stores.

Starbucks was a privately held business from 1987 to 1992. Those years were a critical growth period for the company. Schultz had promised investors in 1987 that Starbucks would open 125 stores in five years. At the end of fiscal 1991, there were 116 stores, all of them in the Northwest or the Chicago area. Starbucks went public on June 26, 1992, at a price of $17 a share and closed that day at $21.50. Starbucks Corporation's common stock still trades on NASDAQ with the ticker symbol SBUX. By the end of fiscal 1992, Schultz had exceeded his original goal. There were 165 Starbucks stores. That year the company expanded to San Francisco, San Diego, Orange County, and Denver.

Since the company went public, the growth has been explosive. Today there are over 32,000 Starbucks stores across the United States and around the world. In 1996, Starbucks expanded overseas. The company set the playing field for global growth by opening its first stores in Japan and Singapore, and today Starbucks is an international brand name found in eighty-three countries around the world. Its net revenues stand at over $23 billion.

Lest you suppose that Starbucks just sells coffee and coffee beverages, think again. Through the years, Starbucks has gradually added cold blended beverages, teas, baked goods, a variety of fresh foods, and, for your listening pleasure, even a selection of music from Spotify. In addition to its company-operated and licensed stores, Starbucks now operates six high-end Roastery locations across the globe that sell rare coffees, complete with an immersive education on the coffee roasting process. Since Starbucks entered into a global alliance with Nestlé in 2018, the companies have launched twenty-four new products, including the widely popular Starbucks creamers such as Caramel Macchiato, White Chocolate Mocha, and Cinnamon Dolce Latte, available in the refrigerated dairy aisle as of 2019. In 2020, the plant-based alternatives, Almondmilk Honey Flat White and Coconutmilk Latte, joined the menu and in 2021, the superfood kale entered with Kale and Portabella Mushroom Sous Vide Egg Bites.

Did You Know?

With over $26 billion in 2019 revenues, Starbucks is roughly 40 times larger than the nation's second largest specialty coffee company—Dunkin' (often referred to as a coffee/donut company).

Dunkin' began in 1950 and has $673 million in annual revenues. They have 9,630 stores scattered over forty-three states and 3,507 international locations in fifty-one countries. In late 2020, Dunkin' was purchased by Inspire Brands, Inc., a multibrand restaurant company that brings a level of expertise that will likely drive further growth for Dunkin' across the globe.

Arabica versus Robusta Beans

There are two types of coffee beans: *Coffea arabica* (arabica) and *Coffea canephora* (robusta). Starbucks buys only the highest-quality arabica beans in the world and then roasts them to the preferred flavor for each variety. Arabica beans are definitely more expensive, but Starbucks continues to buy only the best arabica coffee it can find. What is the difference?

Arabica coffee accounts for approximately 75 percent of the world's coffee production. It is grown at higher altitudes and thrives in shade. In fact, the higher the altitude, the more flavorful the bean. The taste is more refined, with a milder flavor. Arabica beans can be dark roasted for a bold, flavorful taste. It is the superior-quality bean and thus carries a premium price.

Robusta, as the name suggests, is a hardier coffee plant and has more resistance to extreme weather conditions. Robusta trees can grow in direct sunlight. Once the beans are ground and brewed, robusta coffee is known for its high caffeine content and harsh taste. This bean thrives at lower elevations, is easy to grow, and thus is less expensive. Most canned coffee uses the inferior robusta bean, which maximizes profit while minimizing flavor. Robusta beans can't be dark roasted; they will burn and become bitter.

During the Brazilian frost of 1994, coffee prices skyrocketed. Starbucks executives realized that by purchasing lower-quality robusta beans, the company could maintain its profit margins (the difference between sales and expenses). Even better, they knew that most customers would probably not notice a blending of high-quality arabica beans with lower-quality robusta. What would you have done—gone for higher profits at the expense of quality? The risk, of course, would be that true coffee aficionados would notice and shun Starbucks, thereby denting the company's stellar reputation. Or would you have continued to use only the best-quality coffee?

The company remained true to its vision. It was and is dedicated to using only the best-quality beans available—100 percent high-quality arabica beans. Schultz concedes that probably fewer than 10 percent of the company's customers would have noticed, yet the leaders chose not to tarnish the Starbucks name.

CHAPTER TWO

The Founders and Early Management Team

For my part, I saw Starbucks not for what it was, but for what it could be.
—Howard Schultz, Chairman Emeritus Starbucks,
Pour Your Heart into It (1997)

Starbucks was founded in Seattle in 1971, not by big-business moguls, but by a trio of friends—Gordon Bowker, Jerry Baldwin, and Zev Siegl. All dreamed of sharing their love of high-quality arabica coffee beans with the people of Seattle. By 1981, that dream had grown into four Seattle locations and a strong wholesale business selling coffee to business and restaurant accounts. Yet, little is mentioned or noticed of the original founders today. In fact, when corporate Starbucks celebrated its thirtieth anniversary in 2001 with reminiscences, coffee, and cake, none of the three was invited. Even so, Starbucks owes much to its founding visionaries who set out on a mission to improve people's lives with the aroma and taste of dark-roasted coffee beans.

Gordon Bowker

The seed of Starbucks can really be attributed to cofounder Gordon Bowker—both the name and the company idea. In 1970, Bowker was a writer in Seattle making once-a-month jaunts to a coffee roaster called Murchie's in Vancouver, British Columbia. A true coffee connoisseur, Bowker found himself bringing back increasingly large loads of coffee with each 140-mile trek north. The coffee beans were purchased at first for himself, then for friends, and finally, for friends of friends. On one trip, the U.S. Customs agent gently explained to him the difference between shopping and smuggling. His solution was to start a coffee company.

Bowker shared his idea and brainstormed with friends Jerry Baldwin and Zev Siegl. The three shared similar interests—movies, literature, classical music, good food, wine, and the best coffee—and they were excited by the thought of bringing the best coffees to Seattle and opening a store in their own city. Their philosophy focused on educating their customers about quality coffee; then, the customers could take their coffee purchases home, grind the beans, and brew the grounds for themselves. Starbucks was born in that conversation on the lawn outside Siegl's Magnolia Bluff house.

Bowker's father had died when he was only three months old, leaving his mother to raise him alone. He graduated from O'Dea High School in Seattle and attended the University of San Francisco. Just eight course-hours short of his degree, he quit and did not graduate from college. Instead, Bowker traveled cross-country with friends, including Siegl. He followed that with a tour through Europe, where he acquired a fondness for beer and Italian espresso.

His odd jobs over the next few years included driving taxis, house-sitting, and guiding tours for Seattle Underground. Working as a writer in the late 1960s, a job for which he needed his caffeine fixes, he scripted educational films for a division of King Broadcasting and did freelance work for the original *Seattle* magazine. He also started an advertising company, Heckler Bowker.

Bowker's role during the start-up phase of Starbucks was in marketing. He continued his day job but worked at the store on weekends. He even painted the first Starbucks store.

By the early 1980s, Bowker remained involved as a Starbucks owner, but he devoted more time to his other business ventures. He helped launch *Seattle Weekly* and cofounded the Redhook Ale Brewery.

Today, Bowker is an extremely successful entrepreneur who likes the challenge of launching start-ups. The entrepreneur is the retired cofounder of Redhook Brewery, a well-known craft brewer across the United States. Redhook was founded in 1981 and operates its brewery out of Seattle. It produces beer under a small number of brands including its flagship Redhook ESB, styled after the Extra Special Bitters found in English pubs. Redhook's beers are distributed nationally, available at both restaurants and stores.

After Bowker and Baldwin sold their Starbucks assets to Howard Schultz and his investor group in 1987, Bowker left the coffee business for a few years. He re-emerged in the caffeinated arena in 1994 and served on the board of Peet's Coffee & Tea from 1994 until May 2008. Peet's, a specialty coffee retailer and roaster, has been owned by Luxembourg-based conglomerate JAB Holding Company since 2012. Based in Emeryville, California, the company has 240 stores nationwide—most located on the West Coast—and opened its first international location in 2017 in Shanghai, China. Peet's is famous for freshness and brews its drip coffee every 30 minutes in order to serve the most savory cup.

Bowker lives in Seattle, and his best friend remains Starbucks cofounder Jerry Baldwin.

Did You Know?

The world's five largest producers of coffee are Brazil, Vietnam, Colombia, Indonesia, and Ethiopia. The United States is the world's largest importer of coffee.

Jerry Baldwin

Gerald "Jerry" Baldwin is a coffee man through and through. He was born in San Francisco and attended the University of San Francisco, where he roomed with Bowker and became friends with Siegl. Following college, Baldwin was an English teacher in the U.S. Army at Fort Ord in California. After his army stint, he and Siegl developed many business ideas, including shooting a series of film documentaries about ethnic music and starting a radio station featuring classical music, but none of their ideas came to fruition. It was not until Bowker brought up his frustration with the difficulties of finding good coffee that everything clicked. Baldwin's business life from that day forward was centered on coffee.

Alfred Peet introduced Baldwin to the fine art of coffee selecting, blending, and roasting in the early 1970s. He became an expert roaster, first with Starbucks and then with Peet's. He is an honorary member of the Kilimanjaro Specialty Coffee Growers Association, a director and past president of the Association Scientifique Internationale du Café, and a former trustee of the Coffee Quality Institute. In addition, Baldwin was a founding director of Redhook Ale Brewery. He was honored with the Lifetime Achievement Award by the Specialty Coffee Association of America, of which he is a past director. He is also a director of TechnoServe, a nonprofit association working to eliminate poverty in Latin America and Africa.

Baldwin was the company's first roaster and served as president of Starbucks until 1987, when the assets were sold to Schultz and his investors. Baldwin and his cofounders also developed other Starbucks spin-off companies. Blue Anchor, for grocery market distribution, was sold to Milestone in 1981. Caravali Coffee, Starbucks' wholesale division, was sold in 1987 at the same time as Starbucks.

With the sale of Starbucks, Baldwin still wanted to remain in the coffee business and decided to retain Peet's Coffee & Tea. He had fallen in love with the Peet's stores years before. Peet's, according to Baldwin, was the ultimate coffee experience. When he learned of the opportunity to buy Peet's in 1984, he was ecstatic. It was a long-held dream. The story goes that he quickly called Bowker to let him know that they were buying Peet's—no discussion. Bowker agreed that Peet's had the best coffee and provided a special place for customers to gather, so there was no argument from him.

Some of Baldwin's disenchantment with Starbucks no doubt came from disagreements with Schultz. Even before he was hired, Baldwin had misgivings about the businessman, and it took more than a year for Schultz to land the job. Baldwin wanted to keep things small, and the ambitious Schultz knew the company was destined for a national presence and then a global one. Baldwin did not go for the espresso bar concept and there was constant stress in Starbucks offices. He was also tired of going back and forth between Peet's and Starbucks, essentially running two companies.

In June 1987, the sale of Starbucks was complete, and any friendship between Baldwin and Schultz was beyond repair. Baldwin departed for Berkeley to maintain Peet's, leaving the coffeehouse he had helped create to its new CEO.

Since taking over his new business, Baldwin has focused on maintaining the legacy of Peet's as the master coffee roaster and authority it has always been. He works to consider employee involvement and creative thinking and encourages open communication with customers and employees. Baldwin and Peet's Coffee & Tea pride themselves on their loyal base of customers, dubbed *Peetnicks* for their devotion to high-quality, signature blend coffees.

Baldwin was president and CEO of Peet's from 1984 to 1994, and from 1994 to 2001 he served as chairman. When Peet's became a publicly traded company in 2001, he took the title of director, which he still retains even after Peet's was sold to JAB Holding in 2012. Under Baldwin's leadership, Peet's has flourished on its successful business journey by continuing to hand-roast its beans and providing suppliers with the highest-quality product.

Zev Siegl

The family of Zev Siegl was entrenched in the Seattle community. Both his parents were well-known Seattleites. Henry Siegl, his father, was a prominent violinist and concertmaster of the Seattle Symphony Orchestra. His mother, Eleanor Siegl, was a respected educator and founder of Bellevue's Little School. Both passed away in the late 1990s.

Siegl and Bowker met in Seattle in the early 1960s and one summer even traveled cross-country together. Eventually, Siegl, Bowker, and Baldwin all settled in Seattle. After embracing the idea to create a coffee store named Starbucks, the trio decided Siegl would travel to the San Francisco area to investigate potential coffee roasters. Siegl visited several but decided that Peet's Coffee & Tea, which had become a favorite among loyal coffee drinkers since its opening in 1966, would be the best choice. All agreed, and Siegl soon began working in the Berkeley store to learn from Peet, the owner and master coffee roaster. Siegl wanted to learn all he could about coffee making, so he placed himself right in the store. Peet's approach to dark roasting high-quality arabica coffee beans was an inspiration for the founders of Starbucks.

From 1971 to 1980, Siegl worked at Starbucks. Originally a tea drinker in the early 1970s (though he has since converted to espresso), he jumped on the idea of opening a coffee store. He had been looking for an excuse to quit his history teaching position and became Starbucks' first paid employee. Siegl, a people-person who enjoyed his customers, scooped coffee beans while extolling the virtues of quality coffee. He was the retail man and thrived in his position. Then in 1980, citing burnout and wanting to move on to other ventures, Siegl sold his portion of the business to partners Bowker and Baldwin.

For the past four decades, Siegl has busied himself with a wide spectrum of small-business activities. He founded Quartermaine Coffee Roasters, Peerless Pie, McGill Corporation, and Socialbees. Today he shares his knowledge as an international speaker to young entrepreneurs and as a business advisor, consulting with start-up and expanding companies. Siegl is an entrepreneur extraordinaire.

Siegl, Bowker, and Baldwin were a powerful trio who took the simple idea of bringing good coffee to Seattle and created a highly respected local roaster and coffee retailer. The stage was set for Schultz to enter the scene and move Starbucks onto a global voyage.

Did You Know?

WHICH IS THE ONLY U.S. STATE THAT GROWS COFFEE?

Hawaii is the only state within the United States that produces coffee. Coffee is grown on the five major islands in eleven different regions. Excluding experimental plantings or rootstocks for grafting, all coffee grown in the state is 100 percent high-quality arabica coffee.

Source: Hawaii Coffee Association.

Howard Schultz

Ten years after Starbucks first opened, Howard Schultz, a former vice president of U.S. operations for Hammarplast, a Swedish housewares firm, joined the company as the director of marketing and operations. Schultz considered the Starbucks coffee bean stores groundbreaking and set out to convince Baldwin to hire him. He later noted, "At that time, I knew of no other high-end coffee bean stores in New York or any other city" (Schultz and Yang 1997, 39). Schultz's mother urged him not to give up a lucrative, high-powered New York position for a small firm that no one had ever heard of. Despite her concern, in the summer of 1982, Schultz and his wife, Sheri, packed up their car and drove 3,000 miles across the country to join the small coffee company with just five stores. With Schultz's visionary concepts, the wheels were set in motion to lead this local roaster and coffee retailer to become a global coffee empire.

Schultz, who in 2019 earned upward of $30 million a year in executive compensation, had meager beginnings. He was born in 1953 in Brooklyn, New York, and he was raised in subsidized public housing in the Canarsie section of the borough. Schultz's father held a series of blue-collar jobs, from truck driver and cab driver to factory worker. Sometimes he would work two or three jobs just to keep his family afloat. Watching his father's struggles, Schultz was determined to succeed. He attended Canarsie High School, where he excelled in sports and was the quarterback of the football team. Schultz then headed to Northern Michigan University on a football scholarship. He ended up not playing football at all, instead taking on part-time jobs and summer work to pay his college expenses. In 1975, Schultz became the first college graduate in his family.

His first job out of college was as a sales trainee for Xerox. He then went to Hammarplast to work in sales and eventually was promoted to vice president of U.S. operations. Shortly after joining Starbucks in 1983, Schultz made a trip to Milan and experienced the coffeehouses of Italy. They served espresso drinks and provided a social gathering place for customers. He brought that concept back to the three Starbucks owners and they agreed to an experimental espresso bar in one downtown Seattle store. Despite its success, the original founders disagreed with Schultz about what the Starbucks focus and mission should be. They wanted to stick with selling their popular coffee beans. Schultz tried without success to convince Bowker and Baldwin that more money could be made in operating coffeehouses than in targeting the home coffee market.

Schultz left Starbucks to open his own Il Giornale coffeehouse in 1986. In less than a year, Il Giornale had opened three locations, and in 1987, Schultz was given the opportunity to buy out his former employers—including the Starbucks Coffee name. He added the six Starbucks stores to his three Il Giornale stores and kept on growing.

Schultz's career in the new Starbucks company started with his role as chairman and CEO from 1987 to 2000; then, he changed to chairman and chief global strategist from 2000 to 2008. The move from executive to strategist was initiated by Schultz himself, who felt it was time to shift his position and allow the wisdom of others to prevail. Orin Smith followed as CEO until his retirement in 2005. Smith had joined Starbucks as vice president and chief financial officer in 1990, later serving as president and chief operating officer beginning in 1994.

The company went public in 1992. With Schultz at the reins, the company's growth multiplied faster than anyone could have dreamed. At the end of fiscal 1987, there were 17 stores; in 1992, there were 165 and by 2000, there were 3,501 stores. At the end of 2005, the number of stores had topped 10,000, and at the end of fiscal 2008 the company had 16,680 stores worldwide in forty-seven countries.

In 2008, Schultz regained his status as Chairman and CEO of Starbucks after an eight-year hiatus in order to address declining store traffic and depressed sales. He replaced Jim Donald, who had served as CEO since March 2005. Donald, who had previously served as president of the company's North American division, was replaced as part of a mass restructuring effort to help the struggling company rebound. Schultz retained his title as chairman and CEO until 2017, transitioning to executive chairman from 2017 to 2018. When Schultz stepped down from his position as Starbucks CEO, the COO Kevin Johnson replaced him. The Schultz reign ended on June 26, 2018, when he stepped down as chairman and a member of the board, but was honored with the title of Chairman Emeritus.

Clearly, Schultz left his company in good hands and financially well healed. Upon his exit, at the end of fiscal 2018, the company had nearly 30,000 stores in seventy-eight countries. Schultz and his wife, Sheri Kersch Schultz, president of the Schultz Family Foundation, continue to live and enjoy life in the Seattle area. They are parents of two adult children, Jordon Schultz, a sportswriter, and Addison Schultz Hirshberg, a social work clinician.

Did You Know?

HOW DID A SOFTWARE STAR END UP AS THE NEW COFFEE KING?

Kevin Johnson began his career as a software engineer with IBM before moving on to leadership roles with Microsoft and Juniper Networks. He first became affiliated with Starbucks in 2009 when he joined the company's board of directors. After six years of learning the Starbucks culture as a member of the board, Johnson expanded his role in 2015 when he became president and COO. As Schultz transitioned to executive chairman in 2017, Johnson shifted into his current role as president and CEO.

Dave Olsen

Another key player in the early development of Starbucks is Dave Olsen. Olsen, who graduated from Montana State University with a Bachelor of Science degree, has been vital to the stellar growth of the Starbucks Corporation. He has long been a coffee lover and visited coffee bars in the San Francisco Bay Area in the 1970s, including Peet's Coffee & Tea in Berkeley. Olsen bought an espresso machine at Peet's and soon became an espresso fanatic and Peet's devotee.

In 1975, he moved to Seattle with the idea of opening his own espresso bar. He soon opened Café Allegro, which was a small coffee bar in the University District, located in the garage of a former mortuary. It was near the University of Washington campus and became a hangout for university professors and students. Olsen learned the retail business, spending time behind the counter serving customers as well as hiring and training baristas. He searched for the best coffee beans and found them across town at Starbucks. The roasters at Starbucks helped him develop a custom espresso roast for Café Allegro, which is still sold in Starbucks stores today.

Upon hearing in the mid-1980s that Schultz was leaving Starbucks to establish a new coffeehouse, Olsen called Schultz and said he would like to work for the new company. He was interested in pursuing the Italian coffer bar concept and agreed to work cheap, starting with a salary of only $12,000 a year. He joined Il Giornale in 1986 and stayed through the transition to Starbucks Corporation. Olsen was soon responsible for traveling to find the best coffee beans in the world. Schultz noted: "Starbucks would not be what it is today if Dave Olsen hadn't been part of my team back at Il Giornale. He shaped its values, bringing a strong, romantic love for coffee, unshakable integrity, disarming honesty, and an insistence on authenticity in every aspect of the business" (Schultz and Yang 1997, 85).

Olsen is committed to giving back to the global community and has helped create programs aimed at improving quality of life for workers in coffee-growing areas of the world. It was in 1999 that Olsen created and led the Social Corporate Responsibility Department for Starbucks. As former senior vice president of Culture and Leadership Development, Olsen retired in 2013, but still serves the company today as a senior advisor.

Alfred Peet (1920–2007)

Coffee pioneer Alfred Peet, founder of Peet's Coffee & Tea, was an inspiration for Starbucks. He passed away on August 29, 2007, at his home in Ashland, Oregon. He was 87 years old and had lived a life devoted to specialty coffees and the unique dark-roasting style he helped make popular. Peet was born in Alkmaar, Holland, on March 10, 1920, the son of a Dutch roaster, and grew up helping his father in the business. After World War II, Peet apprenticed himself to Lipton's Tea in London as a tea taster and then ventured to Indonesia to work in the tea business. In 1955, he moved to San Francisco, where he took a job in the coffee importing industry.

Peet was troubled by the poor quality of coffee being brought into the United States, and hence, the poor coffee Americans were drinking. So, in 1966, Peet decided to open his own shop at Walnut and Vine streets in Berkeley, California. With the opening of that one tiny store, the world of specialty coffee would never be the same. The gourmet coffee trend started on the West Coast and moved east to engulf the nation. Peet used superior-quality coffee beans and hand-roasted them, which gave the coffee its top-quality flavor. A gathering place for coffee connoisseurs, his business was frequented by University of California—Berkeley faculty, students, intellectuals, and writers. The store flourished, and Peet soon opened additional shops in the San Francisco Bay Area. Peet's Coffee & Tea is still in operation today, and the original location is referred to as the Gourmet Ghetto. Today, the company operates 244 retail stores in the United States and 1 in China.

Peet taught others his unique style of roasting beans, which was quite different from that of the mainstream coffee companies. He used superior-quality beans, hand-roasted them in small batches, and developed a dark-roasting style for richer flavor. Young Seattle entrepreneurs Jerry Baldwin, Gordon Bowker, and Zev Siegl asked Peet to provide his roasted coffee beans for their new coffee venture, Starbucks Coffee, Tea, and Spices, in 1971. He also served as a mentor, teaching the new businessmen his roasting technique.

Peet retired in 1983, and just one year later, Starbucks partners Baldwin and Bowker, along with a group of investors, bought Peet's four Bay Area locations. When Baldwin and Bowker sold Starbucks to Howard Schultz and his investors in 1987, Baldwin kept the original Peet's coffee shop, and the business Alfred Peet had started would continue to grow. In 2001, Peet's became a public company, trading on the NASDAQ, and in 2012 was acquired by JAB Holding.

Did You Know?

A coffeehouse sells coffee, coffee-related drinks, and select food items. A coffeehouse is also a social gathering place for customers to connect through conversation. Customers may also read, write, or work at a coffeehouse, while sipping coffee.

Italians are serious about their coffee and often enjoy espresso at a bar, while standing or sitting on a bar stool, hence the term coffee bar. Although today most Starbucks locations have ample seating, comfy chairs, couches, and a relaxed atmosphere, the coffeehouse culture at Starbucks has its origins from the espresso coffee bar.

CHAPTER THREE

The Coffeehouse Experience

Starbucks executives continue to respectfully and willingly share profits with their people. Through this sharing, partners appreciate the direct link between their effort and the success of the business enterprise.
—Joseph A. Michelli, *The Starbucks Experience: 5 Principles for Turning Ordinary into Extraordinary* (2007)

The Shift to Coffee Bars

When Howard Schultz first decided to leave Starbucks in 1986, he was determined to shift away from the focus on retail sales to see his coffee bar vision fulfilled. At the time, Schultz's parting from Starbucks was amicable; the departure was simply the result of a differing vision. Schultz had a goal of re-creating the Italian coffeehouse culture, while Gordon Bowker and Jerry Baldwin were satisfied with the status quo at Starbucks and were not impressed with the experiment that placed espresso machines in their stores. They were dedicated to the old-fashioned retail side of selling coffee by the bag.

So, Schultz moved on and started Il Giornale. The first Il Giornale coffee bar was in the Columbia Seafirst Center, the tallest building in Seattle. Il Giornale thrived, while Starbucks remained at a standstill. Schultz opened another coffee bar shortly thereafter in Seattle and a third one in Vancouver. The relationship between the companies was still cordial, in that Il Giornale sold Starbucks coffee in its stores. Schultz placed Dave Olsen in charge of his store operations.

Meanwhile at Starbucks, morale was down, and people were not happy. There was dissension among the staff; employees felt the management was not behind them anymore. Bowker and Baldwin had grown tired of the hassles created by business growth. The company had moved far beyond the founders' original goal of bringing quality arabica coffee beans to others. Bowker had developed interests in other ventures, and Baldwin's true love was the Peet's Coffee & Tea store. They decided to keep Peet's and put Starbucks up for sale—the Seattle stores, the roasting plant, and the Starbucks name.

When Schultz heard the news, he could not pass up the opportunity to buy the company he felt had so much potential. Schultz got on board with his investors in Il Giornale to the tune of nearly $4 million for the six-unit Starbucks chain. Although the friendship between Schultz and his former employers would soon terminate, they agreed on the sale. In 1987, the Il Giornale shops changed their names to Starbucks and the unified company became Starbucks Corporation. A new Starbucks was born.

After a twenty-month sabbatical developing his own company, 34-year-old Schultz was back with Starbucks, now as president and CEO. Baldwin remained president of the now-separately owned and operated Peet's Coffee & Tea.

That same year, Starbucks began its national expansion boom by opening stores outside Seattle, in Vancouver and in Chicago. Chicago had a particularly tough opening day—the first store opened on the day of the stock market crash—but Chicagoans eventually took to the dark-roasted coffee. Of course, this was after Schultz learned the hard way that the store should not open up directly onto the street. The winter weather is too frigid in Chicago to do so. Chicagoans showed by their patronage that they'd much prefer a store that opened up into a lobby.

Starbucks' rocky beginnings as it expanded its market to new cities eventually turned into phenomenal growth. At the end of fiscal 1987, the Starbucks Corporation had seventeen stores. Visionary Schultz promised investors in 1987 that Starbucks would open 125 stores in five years. The store openings advanced to 33 in 1988, 55 in 1989, 84 in 1990, and 116 in 1991, and in 1992 the goal was exceeded with 165 stores.

At the helm, Schultz was free to incorporate his coffee bar dream into Starbucks. He wanted to re-create a true Italian-style coffee bar. In Italy, the coffee bar is a "third place" between work and home, where people can enjoy coffee and socialize, and this is what Schultz envisioned and made happen for Starbucks. His first coffee bar had a stately espresso machine as its centerpiece, and the bar concept was an instant hit. All service was initially stand-up, with no seating areas. It was quickly discovered, though, that Americans wanted chairs. Nonetheless, the coffee bar environment, with baristas educating consumers on Italian-style espresso, enabled Starbucks' growth to skyrocket.

Did You Know?

In 1987, one of the original Il Giornale investors proposed terms to buy Starbucks himself, and he wanted Howard Schultz to agree to his terms. Fearing that all of his investors might go along with the other proposal, Schultz called in someone with clout to go along with him to the meeting about the proposal.

Can you guess who attended the meeting with Schultz? Bill Gates, Sr., the late father of Microsoft's founder, Bill Gates. The senior Gates was a lawyer, a prestigious Seattleite, and a towering six feet, seven inches tall.

In 1987, original founders Jerry Baldwin and Gordon Bowker sold Starbucks' six retail establishments, roasting plant, and name. Schultz put together an investment group, and every original investor in Il Giornale had an opportunity to invest in the purchase of Starbucks. The Il Giornale investors backed Schultz along with almost all other investors that were approached. The purchase price for Starbucks was $3.8 million. The three-unit Il Giornale acquired the assets of Starbucks and changed its name to Starbucks Corporation. The coffee bar dream was launched, and the rest is history.

The Third Place Concept

Who said you have to be inside a Starbucks retail establishment to get the Third Place coffeehouse experience? Certainly not Starbucks. The company has adapted with the changing culture of advancing technology and busy clientele. Today, the Third Place experience can be adapted with both drive-thru and top-notch delivery options.

Drive-thru service has become commonplace, and Starbucks knows its customers can have a great coffeehouse experience, even on the run. In 2018, Starbucks was watching their drive-thru locations thrive. At the Q4 2018 Earnings Call, Rosalind G. Brewer, Group President, COO, and Director, Starbucks, spilled the tea and addressed the growing need for convenience. Stores with drive-thru well outperformed café-comparable sales, Brewer noted. "And from a U.S. portfolio strategy, more than 80% of our new stores in FY 2018 were drive-thru and this format will be a continued focus into FY 2019." Brewer continued the positive theme at the Q4 2019 Earnings Call, stating, "Additionally, our drive-thru business continues to grow well, and you'll see that continue through fiscal year

2020." The fact that Starbucks had developed a strong drive-thru presence was a strong advantage when COVID-19 hit, as evidenced by the roughly 75 percent of U.S. sales volume in the last quarter of 2020 being drive-thru and mobile orders.

The drive-thru success is not the only sign of our hectic lifestyle shift. Mobile ordering and food delivery options are robust. The highly popular Mobile Order & Pay feature on the Starbucks app allows customers to order online, pick up the order, and bypass the check-out line. Customers may stay in the store for the traditional experience or quickly move back to work or home, thus opting for an abbreviated coffeehouse experience. Meal delivery is the global trend, and Starbucks is riding the convenience wave. Along with widespread delivery options in the United States, Starbucks offers delivery in over 15 global markets. The online food delivery service is forecast to continue on an upward spiral, perhaps redefining the Third Place to the Digital Place.

Quality Specialty Coffee

Top-quality, fresh-roasted, whole-bean coffee was, and is, the company's foundation. Peet's use of high-grade arabica beans, dark roasted by a trained roaster, became the focus for Starbucks. Baldwin was the first roaster for Starbucks. The company uses costly methods but produces a trademark beverage. Since 1971, Starbucks has been driven to ethically source and roast the uppermost-quality arabica beans in the world. The company is both the world's leading roaster and leading retailer of specialty coffee. Roasting and sourcing its own beans allow the company to tightly control the quality of its product.

Starbucks coffee buyers make it their mission to select only the highest-quality arabica beans. Buyers travel the world—largely to Latin America, Africa, and Asia/Pacific—to select beans. Then, roasters take the beans and develop the rich, dark roast that is Starbucks' trademark. Currently, Starbucks has five established roasting plants: in Washington State, Pennsylvania, Nevada, South Carolina, and Amsterdam. A small portion of the beans ends up in Starbucks Reserve Roasteries as well.

First, green coffee beans are fired in a large, rotating drum. The first audible pop will occur after roughly 8 minutes in the roaster. The beans increase in size, roughly doubling. The coffee beans are now light brown in color. After 10–11 minutes in the roaster, the coffee beans become an even brown color. Usually, somewhere between 11 and 15 minutes in, the full flavor potential begins to build up in the beans. The listener will hear a second crack, which is really a group of forceful crackling noises. The dark roast begins, and the great Starbucks flavor develops at the second crack.

Starbucks Reserve

The ultimate coffeehouse experience, with premier high-end coffee, takes place at one of the six Starbucks Reserve Roastery locations. The first Reserve Roastery opened in Seattle in 2014, just nine blocks from the original Starbucks location. All Starbucks Reserve Roastery facilities roast on location as well as package and serve the specialty small lot coffee. It is a total immersive educational experience, with customers viewing the roasting process along with a bit of education from baristas on coffee techniques and brewing processes. Along with Seattle, Roastery locations include Shanghai, Milan, New York, Tokyo, and Chicago.

A more intimate coffeehouse experience is offered at the Starbucks Reserve Coffee Bars, which currently number forty-three across the globe. One of the largest Reserve Coffee Bars, Starbucks Reserve SODO, is located on the ground floor of Starbucks headquarters in Seattle. Relaxation and chit-chat with one of the many knowledgeable baristas is paramount at these coffee bars. Brewing methods have a major impact on the way coffee tastes, so a coffee bar provides a great opportunity for customers to take away some tips to help with their coffee brewing ritual. Customers may also find the limited-quantity Starbucks Reserve coffee at 1,500-plus Starbucks locations around the world. The notable star and the R logo will help you identify a Reserve Roastery, a Reserve Coffee Bar, and Starbucks Reserve coffee.

The coffees in the Reserve program are distinctive, and all have a unique story to tell. For example, Vietnam Da Lat captures the flavors of "toffee, kola nuts, and cocoa peel" grown in the remote area of Vietnam's Central Highlands. We learn that farmers typically motor-bike the freshly picked beans to buying stations. Columbia Pedregal, with "flavors reminiscent of pear and red apple with a panela sweetness," comes from coffee trees that thrive in volcanic soil. Hawaii Ka'u has a "creamy milk chocolate flavor with an almond sweetness" and is grown on the south side of the Big Island. Read the following interview with Chris Manfredi, President of the Hawaii Coffee Association, to learn about the history, growth, and future of the Ka'u coffee region.

Coffee Talk: *An Interview with Chris Manfredi, President of the Hawaii Coffee Association*

According to the Hawaii Coffee Association, the common belief is that coffee first arrived in the island in 1825 from Brazil, planted in the Mānoa valley on the island of O'ahu. Growing coffee in the early decades in Hawaii was challenging as plantations fought insects and harsh weather conditions and endured competition for land and labor from the sugar plantations. Of all the early commercial ventures, Kona on the Big Island is the only region that has remained in continual production.

In 1892, a new coffee was introduced to Hawaii from Guatemala. The new Guatemalan coffee was a more prolific crop, and farmers quickly gravitated away from the Brazilian variety. In the 1980s, when sugarcane was no longer profitable, many of the sugarcane fields migrated to coffee. Today, more farms grow coffee than any other crop in the state. Coffee has moved into eleven major regions on five different islands, with one of the major regions being Ka'u.

Hawaii Ka'u joined the Starbucks Reserve program in 2011 to rave reviews. The coffee, from the Ka'u region on the south side of the Big Island, has skyrocketed to worldwide fame over the last decade. In its early years, growers were mostly selling Ka'u in the Kona coffee market, but all that changed in 2007 when Ka'u coffee entered the Specialty Coffee Association of America's annual cupping competition and earned Coffee of the Year honors. In the years following, Ka'u coffee consistently placed in the top ten coffees in competitions internationally. With notoriety, an earned unique identity, and the assistance of Chris Manfredi of Ka'u Farm and Ranch Co., Starbucks took notice of this award-winning coffee and brought it onboard to its elite Reserve selection.

The Hawaii Coffee Association, a trade association representing all sectors of the coffee industry including growers, millers, wholesalers, and retailers, educates and promotes Hawaiian coffee. Chris Manfredi, now President of the Hawaii Coffee Association, discusses the history, growth, and future of the Ka'u coffee region.

HOW DID COFFEE COME TO THE KA'U REGION?

In Ka'u, sugar was everything, and if not sugar, cattle ranching. It was a way of life. Farmers were generationally dependent on the sugar plantations. The plantation provided essentially everything—schools, housing, stores, and theaters.

When the Ka'u sugar plantation closed in 1996, some farmers turned to coffee. The plantation offered their former employees affordable leases to get started, but the growers experienced increasingly thin margins and many farms were later abandoned. In those days, the crop was largely sold into the Kona market, with the Kona buyers telling the growers their coffee wasn't very good. After winning the first awards, and a renewed sense of community pride, more farmers started to grow coffee and renovate the farms. Because the land was previously used for sugar cane crops, it was not initially suitable for growing coffee, and many challenges occurred. But now people are coming to Ka'u to start farms. It has been a remarkable turnaround. Initially, there was no sense of home ownership—plantation worker housing was in the form of plantation camps. These are now private homes occupied by the former planation workers as independent businessmen and women. Today, growers are paid more than four times what they earned when selling their crop to Kona buyers.

HOW DID YOU GET INTO THE COFFEE BUSINESS?

I was a mechanic and entrepreneur from an early age and intimately involved in professional motor sports, which taught me many skills about preparation, vision, balance, and teamwork that would help me in future endeavors. Initially, I went to Hawaii on vacation, but my entrepreneurial propensity led me to an opportunity in real estate and ended up buying 6,000 acres of former sugar plantation land that included 270 acres of coffee farms. The forty or so coffee farmers were my tenants.

Because I came from a background of auto racing where competition is the core of the sport, I thought let's put the coffee into competition to see if it's good or bad. In 2007, I sent Ka'u coffee to the Specialty Coffee Association of American's Roasters Guild Coffee of the Year Competition. The coffee placed 6th and 9th out of more than 100 entrants. That first year we had zero preparation. I was just looking for a baseline. Since then Ka'u coffee has built an extraordinary reputation and earned numerous awards. Ka'u started to develop an identity of its own, being evaluated by third-party professionals. In 2012, Ka'u notably received three of the top ten Coffee of the Year awards.

CAN YOU TELL READERS HOW KA'U CAME TO THE ATTENTION OF STARBUCKS?

Ka'u started to have its own name recognition with the notoriety of awards. In 2010, I brought it to Starbucks attention and the following year, Hawaii Ka'u entered the Reserve Program. It was a combination of outstanding quality, perseverance, and a little luck.

HOW WOULD YOU DESCRIBE THE TASTE OF HAWAII KA'U COFFEE?

There are many descriptors to describe Ka'u coffee—it is a well-balanced cup and it varies lot to lot and farm to farm. Some of the descriptors used are chocolate, cherry, cedar, orchid, and citrus notes.

WHAT DOES THE FUTURE LOOK LIKE FOR HAWAII KA'U?

It is a general upward trend, and a work in progress. We are still in the early stages of our development as an origin. Ours is a vibrant and more resilient agricultural community that helps fill the void left by the plantation system.

In 2009, Manfredi organized the first Ka'u Coffee Festival, now an annual tradition featuring a Ka'u Coffee Recipe Contest, Ka'u Coffee and Cattle Day, Ka'u Star Gazing, and many more activities. The mission of the festival is to raise awareness of Ka'u as a world-class coffee growing origin and visitor destination. Participants can even attend the annual Ka'u Coffee College, an educational and networking event featuring leaders in the specialty coffee industry from around the globe. Check out Kaucoffeefestival.com for details.

Ka'u Growing Region Fun Facts

1. There are eighty to ninety coffee farms.
2. The growing area is 830 acres.
3. Elevation is 1,100–2,700 feet.
4. The district of Ka'u spans the south side of the Big Island of Hawaii.
5. The unique climate produces some of the best-specialty coffees of the world.

Source: Hawaii Coffee Association, *Grown with Aloha,* 2018.

Entertainment by Starbucks

What could make your coffee experience even better? Free Wi-Fi is a given and is necessary in today's high-tech work-and-play environment. Starbucks was early to the game; in 2008 Starbucks added Wi-Fi in stores with limited access and, in 2010, moved to free, unlimited access.

Starbucks believes listening to great music while sipping its coffee heightens your enjoyment. In a Starbucks Stories press release dated January 19, 2016, the company acknowledges the connection, stating, "For more than four decades, Starbucks has built a differentiated Third Place experience with music at the heart of its coffeehouse culture." While in-house music has long been a part of the Starbucks coffeehouse scene, in 2016 Starbucks took it to a new level by launching a digital music experience with streaming service Spotify. Starbucks handpicks favorite artists and songs from around the globe, and Starbucks Mobile App users are now able to discover music playing overhead at participating stores. App users can view recently played songs and even save songs to a personal playlist on Spotify. Customers can also find new playlists as well as Starbucks' most popular music from the past twenty years on Spotify.

Store Ownership and Expansion

Starbucks stores are located in urban, suburban, and even some rural areas. Convenience is an important part of their strategy, so Starbucks provides customers with convenience by providing plentiful drive-thru opportunities and off-highway stores.

For much of the history of Starbucks, *franchising* was almost a dirty word in company ranks. Franchising is a form of business expansion in which the owner of a product or service authorizes someone else to sell or distribute that company's goods or services, in return for monetary compensation. Although franchising is a common strategy for many firms that want quick national growth, Schultz was opposed to the business strategy for many years. He wrote, "If we had franchised, Starbucks would have lost the common culture that made us strong" (Schultz and Yang 1997, 173). But in 1991, the opportunity became too tempting and an exception was made. Schultz concedes: "The opportunities to attract new customers were too appealing to pass up, and the window would not be open indefinitely. Each new venture, though, is part of an ongoing struggle."

The first big concession was in the airport arena. Seattle opened its first licensed airport store with HMHS Host, starting in Seattle and expanding to airports across the United States. The relationship is still going strong as HMHS Host is the exclusive provider of Starbucks coffee in airports in North America. Starbucks works with carefully selected businesses to operate licensed stores in a number of different types of establishments. Today you might find Starbucks in select grocery stores, hotels, food-service companies, hospitals, churches, libraries, and military bases. The leadership team is very careful about the companies chosen to license the Starbucks name.

At the end of fiscal 2020, out of the 32,660 locations, there were 16,023 licensed stores and 16,637 company-operated stores. The mix of company-operated versus licensed stores depends on numerous factors including the specific market, the ability to access prime retail space, profitability, and complexity. At the 2019 annual meeting, Kevin Johnson noted: "Now, we've streamlined the company across four dimensions, retail market alignment. We've transitioned a number of markets around the world to our licensed partners. Why? Because they'll grow that market faster than we would as a company operated model." It is a wise strategy to be flexible with owning or licensing, and although it typically is more profitable with corporate ownership, partnering with a licensee may provide essential expertise in an area, as well as access to prime real estate.

Employees working in Starbucks licensed locations attend training classes similar to those attended by baristas working at the company-operated stores. The good news is that customers receive the same level of coffee expertise and customer service at all Starbucks locations, whether company owned or licensed. If customers are traveling through the airport, staying at a hotel, shopping, or visiting a hospital, they will likely find a Starbucks establishment along the way. Licensed options provide individuals a high likelihood of being able to re-create the coffeehouse experience that provides them coffee and comfort.

Starbucks began its overseas expansion in 1996, starting in Tokyo. Adding to its growing international influence, in 1998 the Starbucks Corporation acquired the Seattle Coffee Company of Britain. Its sixty stores were given the Starbucks name, and the company had an instant presence in that country. The company now has over 32,000 coffeehouses in eighty-three countries around the globe. Table 3.1 shows the countries where Starbucks has a presence of licensed stores, and Table 3.2 shows the company-operated store data. The company's development strategy adapts to different international markets, staying aware of local needs.

While its main goal is protecting the quality of Starbucks coffee, the company is adaptable to cultural issues, social norms, and taste. There are 1,464 stores in Japan, but adaptations were made. Stores there provide green tea Frappuccinos, smaller cup sizes, and smaller pastries to suit the Japanese preferences. Asian markets have more savory foods to adapt to different tastes. The Shanghai Roastery features a Teavana Tea Bar, a modern tea experience designed uniquely for Chinese customers, honoring their long-held tea tradition and love of tea.

Table 3.1   Starbucks Licensed Stores around the World
(Stores Open as of September 27, 2020)

Americas:	
United States	6,387
Mexico	752
Latin America	662
Canada	444
Total Americas	8,245
International:	
Korea	1,468
United Kingdom	737
Turkey	530
Taiwan	501
Indonesia	458
Philippines	396
Thailand	405
All others	3,283
Total International	7,778
TOTAL LICENSED	16,023

Source: Starbucks 10-K 2020.

Table 3.2   Starbucks Company-Operated Stores around the
World (Stores Open as of September 27, 2020)

Americas:	
United States	8,941
Canada	1,159
Siren Retail	9
Total Americas	10,109
International:	
China	4,704
Japan	1,464
United Kingdom	288
All others	67
Siren Retail	5
Total International	6,528
TOTAL COMPANY-OPERATED	16,637

Source: Starbucks 10-K 2020.

You Decide

Is one person worth a multimillion-dollar compensation in a company? Kevin Johnson, current president and CEO of Starbucks, is highly valued by his board. The year 2020 was good for Johnson with a total compensation topping $14 million. Most of his pay was earned from stock awards, options, and incentive pay; nonetheless, his base salary for that year was still $1.5 million.

If you were a board member and had the responsibility of deciding the CEO's salary, what would you do? Is it prudent to approve such a high compensation package for Johnson? Is anyone worth $14 million a year to a company? One school of thought says high salaries are needed to retain top-quality executives to run profitable mega-corporations. Others think such salaries are excessive and greedy, and the funds could be better utilized to provide returns to shareholders, higher salaries for all employees, or lower prices for consumers. This is a subject where the experts disagree, and there are probably no right or wrong answers. Which side are you on?

Coffee, Tea, and More

Starbucks is known for its world-class arabica coffee, but if java is not your thing, the Starbucks coffeehouse experience will probably still appeal to you. There is a tasty drink or treat for everyone. Tea lovers enjoy the wide variety of Teavana teas. The company has fine accessories galore: espresso machines, coffeemakers, coffee presses, grinders, tea presses, tea kettles, and more. You would rather just have water? In its coffeehouses, Starbucks sells Ethos bottled water. Ethos Water not only quenches thirst but also has a social mission of helping children around the world get clean water. Hungry? Starbucks sells salads, sandwiches, breakfast items, snacks, and pastries in select markets. Don't forget to look in the grocery store for coffee, tea, ice cream, and cold drinks. Check out the informative Starbucks Products sidebar for a detailed listing of products.

Starbucks Products

Coffee: More than thirty blends and single-origin premium coffees.

Handcrafted Beverages: Fresh-brewed coffee, hot and iced espresso beverages, Iced Coffee, Cold Brew, Nitro, Frappuccino® coffee and noncoffee blended beverages, Starbucks Refreshers® beverages, and Teavana® teas.

Merchandise: Coffee- and tea-brewing equipment, mugs and accessories, packaged goods, books, and gifts.

Fresh Food: Baked pastries, cold and hot sandwiches, salads, salad and grain bowls, oatmeal, yogurt parfaits, and fruit cups.

Consumer products available where groceries are sold:

- **Coffee and Tea:** Whole-bean and ground coffee (Starbucks and Seattle's Best Coffee brands), Starbucks VIA® Instant, Starbucks espresso capsules available on the Nespresso and Nescafé Dolce Gusto systems, Starbucks® Coffee K-Cup® pods, Starbucks® and Teavana® Verismo® pods.

- **Ready-to-Drink (RTD):** Starbucks® bottled Frappuccino® coffee drinks, Starbucks Iced Latte, Single Serve Cold Brew, Doubleshot® Coffee Smoothies, Teavana Craft Iced Teas, Teavana Sparkling Craft Iced Teas, Starbucks Discoveries® chilled cup coffees, Starbucks Discoveries Iced Café Favorites®, Starbucks Iced Coffee, Starbucks Doubleshot® espresso drinks, Starbucks Doubleshot® Energy Coffee drinks; Starbucks Refreshers® beverages, Evolution Fresh™ bottled juices.

Source: Starbucks Company Profile (https://www.starbucks.com/about-us/company-information/starbucks-company-profile). Retrieved December 15, 2019.

The company stays current in today's world by continuing to roll out amazing new business agreements that create wonderful new treats. In 2018, Nestlé paid Starbucks $7.2 billion to market, sell, and distribute Starbucks packaged coffees and teas globally, outside of the retail coffee stores. Nestlé is the world's largest food and beverage company, known for Nescafe and Nespresso in the coffee business, and its global distribution power will aid in selling Starbucks coffee and tea products around the world. Two years later, the Global Alliance with Nestlé has expanded the internationally in-home coffee presence of Starbucks, now in sixty-two markets.

Did You Know?

Coffee contains caffeine, which is a stimulant. Because coffee can provide a boost of energy, some people enjoy a cup or two to start their day. Still others might sip coffee as a pick-me-up later in the afternoon. Employees working the third shift can usually find a pot of coffee brewing to help them stay alert. Truck drivers may drink coffee to keep them awake during long trips. Even students, studying late into the night, may down a cup of coffee or two to help in a late-night study session.

But too much caffeine can raise your blood pressure, increase your heart rate, cause irritability, and keep you from sleeping. If you enjoy the taste of coffee but it simply makes you too jumpy, you do have an alternative. Decaffeinated coffee is a great option because decaffeination involves removing caffeine from coffee. Decaf is produced with products that extract the caffeine from the coffee beans. So, if you find coffee to be too invigorating, try one of the many decaf whole-bean or ground coffee varieties available.

CHAPTER FOUR

Behind the Blends

We're going to dedicate to building that future for farmers to ensure the future of coffee and the economic livelihood of farmers is protected for many generations to come. We are playing the long game.
—Michelle Burns, Senior Vice President-Global Coffee & Tea,
Starbucks, *Annual Meeting* (March 20, 2019)

The best conditions for coffee to grow occur in a belt that surrounds the globe, between the Tropic of Capricorn and the Tropic of Cancer, commonly referred to as the Coffee Belt. Even in the Coffee Belt, conditions must be just right to produce the high-quality arabica coffee that is sourced by Starbucks. The coffee trees that produce arabica grow well in higher altitudes, 3,000–6,000 feet above sea level and with mild temperatures in the range of 18–21 degrees Celsius. The lower-quality and less-flavorful robusta is a stronger plant, requiring less care than its arabica counterpart. Robusta is commonly found in the Eastern Hemisphere; can thrive at lower altitudes, higher temperatures; and is more resistant to insects and disease.

With great care comes great reward, and for the milder, more sophisticated arabica coffee Starbucks takes exceptional care with the farming to the cup process. Starbucks purchases 3 percent of the world's coffee, which is sourced from over 400,000 farmers. For decades, the buyers have been traveling to remote farming destinations, commonly in Latin America, Asia/Pacific, and Africa. So what is the company doing to protect the farmers who grow this delicate coffee and ensure that the arabica coffee bean will be available in the future? The farmer support centers provide major assistance and educational tools.

Farmer Support Centers

In 2001, the company began developing its socially responsible coffee buying guidelines called C.A.F.E. practices (Coffee and Farmer Equity Practices). The coffee verification program was officially launched in 2004, the same year the company opened its first farmer support center in San José, Costa Rica. The program ensures that Starbucks coffee is ethically sourced, developed in concert with Conservation International (CI), a nonprofit environmental organization. "Committed to 100% Ethical Coffee Sourcing in partnership with Conservation International" is printed on Starbucks coffee packaging, exemplifying the company's commitment to farmers and the entire coffee community.

As of 2015, the company reached and has maintained a level of 99 percent of its coffee chain as ethically sourced. C.A.F.E. practices are more exhaustive than the well-known Fair-Trade certification, which carries general social, economic, and environmental standards. Described by the company news release in a recent publication (C.A.F.E. Practices: Starbucks Approach to Ethically Sourcing Coffee, February 28, 2020), C.A.F.E. is

> a verification program that measures farms against economic, social and environmental criteria, all designed to promote transparent, profitable and sustainable coffee growing practices while also protecting the well-being of coffee farmers and workers their families and their communities. C.A.F.E. Practices has helped Starbucks create a long-term supply of high-quality coffee and positively impact the lives and livelihoods of coffee farmers and their communities.

Third-party organizations oversee the process, making inspections at farms, mills, and warehouses throughout the supply chain and scoring over 200 performance indicators.

In nearly a two-decade period, Starbucks has amassed a total of eight traditional Farmer Support Centers (see Table 4.1) plus an agronomy center in Hacienda Alsacia, which is the Starbucks coffee farm. The original Costa Rica Farmer Support Center relocated from downtown San José to the Hacienda Alsacia property in 2016. The nine centers assist the farmers with education and hands-on help working with individuals in the field in order to improve both the quality and the profitability of the coffee crop.

The 2019 Annual Report explains the purpose:

> To help ensure the future supply of high-quality green coffee and to reinforce our leadership role in the coffee industry, Starbucks operates nine farmer support centers. The farmer support centers are staffed with agronomists and sustainability experts who work with coffee farming communities to promote best practices in coffee production designed to improve both coffee quality and yields and agronomy support to address climate and other impacts.

Farmers are able to glean information and collaborate with highly trained agronomists, scientists who study soil management and growing and harvesting crops.

The Farmer Support Centers are positively impacting many who work the soil, with a goal of training 200,000 farmers by 2020. Currently, over 160,000 farmers have been trained at the farming centers and agronomy center. Examples of coffee training education include methodologies for fertilization, spacing trees appropriately, and performing soil tests. Lessons on erosion management and pesticide use are also vital. With such specialized coffee education, knowledge will lead to a healthier coffee crop while increasing the standard of living for the farmer. It is a win for both the company and the farmer.

Table 4.1   Starbucks Farmer Support Centers

(Location: Opening Date)

San José, Costa Rica: 2004 (relocated to Hacienda Alsacia in 2016)

Guatemala City, Guatemala (Satellite): 2006

Kigali, Rwanda: 2009

Mbeya, Tanzania: 2011

Manizales, Colombia: 2012

Yunnan, China: 2012

Addis Ababa, Ethiopia: 2014

North Sumatra, Indonesia: 2015

Chiapas, Mexico: 2016

Source: Starbucks Stories & News, *Starbucks Farmer Support Centers,* March 7, 2018.

Hacienda Alsacia

Coffee is important to the economy of Costa Rica and one of the country's top ten exports, thus many farmers rely on the crop for their livelihood. In 2013, Starbucks bought a coffee farm, Hacienda Alsacia, in Costa Rica, a 240-hectare (593-acres) property. The farm, located at the foot of Poás Volcano, was in dilapidated condition upon purchase but within a few years it was an exemplary working model for the small farmer. Starbucks targeted the property as the company's global agronomy headquarters with the mission of assisting the small farmer, even if the farmer does not grow coffee for Starbucks. The objective is simple: to assist the entire coffee community.

On Hacienda Alsacia's website, www.starbuckscoffeefarm.com, the goal of the farm is clear: "To help ensure the future of coffee, the mission of Hacienda Alsacia is clear: Create best practices to make growing coffee more profitable for small-scale farms; develop the next generation of disease-resistant, quality coffee; and share it all with farmers around the world." Not only is the coffee farm a research and development facility for the company, it is a working farm, one in which people can visit and experience.

The coffee-curious may learn how coffee beans are grown, picked, milled, dried, and roasted at the Hacienda Alsacia Visitor Center. Opened in 2018, the 46,000-square-foot center provides an immersive experience from "soil to cup." In a 90-minute tour, visitors see how Starbucks is supporting farmers with the development of new hybrid coffee trees, more resistant to diseases and climate change. Visitors leave with a fresh cup of coffee from the farm. For those unable to travel to Costa Rica for a live tour, virtual visitors may explore the website and read about the coffee journey, while sipping on a Decaf Costa Rica Hacienda Alsacia small-lot Reserve coffee and experiencing the "sparkling acidity balanced by citrus and milk chocolate flavors."

The Role of an Agronomist

An agronomist is a technical expert in soil management and crop production. A commonly known slang for an agronomist is a crop doctor, and Starbucks employs many of the scientists who have concern for the health and development of the coffee crop. At Starbucks, the director of Global Agronomy is Carlos Mario Rodriguez, who has held that position since 2004, currently overseeing all of the Farmer Support Centers and leading all research at Hacienda Alsacia. The work of Rodriguez is widely recognized, being named one of the "Most Creative People in Business" in 2016 by Fast Company. A major accomplishment, Rodriguez and his team

have developed research on hybrid trees and practice open-source agronomy, sharing information and research with the coffee community. Starbucks donates the hybrid trees to farms suffering from diseases like coffee
rust, a powerful leaf rust that resembles an orange rusty powder which
can devastate a coffee crop.

Farmers

At the heart of the company are the 400,000 farmers in twenty-eight
countries who grow the coffee beans that Starbucks purchases. Starbucks
supports the farmers not only through education but also with a premium
price for their high-quality arabica coffee. Contracts are finalized years
ahead, a practice which reduces volatility and allows more stability to the
farmer's income. In addition to the Farmer Support Centers, farmers are
supported in a multitude of ways, including the Plant a Tree programs,
the Global Farmer Fund, Emergency Relief Fund, Option Grants, and
productive partnerships.

Plant a Tree

Farmers count on a certain amount of coffee cherries to sell each year
for their livelihood. The problem? Coffee rust is a significant detrimental
issue along with aging trees, which produce much less. It takes a sizable
amount of coffee cherries to produce a pound of coffee. According to Starbucks, one coffee tree produces only enough cherries for one pound of
coffee, and aging and trees impacted by disease will produce much less
(*Starbucks Stories*. "22 Million Coffee Trees from Starbucks 'One Tree for
Every Bag'." Starbucks Coffee Company, December 2, 2016).

In September 2015, Starbucks launched its One Tree for Every Bag
commitment in honor of National Coffee Day (typically celebrated on September 29 in the United States). The goal, as the plan hints, was to plant
one tree for each bag of coffee purchased in U.S. Starbucks stores through
the end of 2016 to replace declining or diseased trees. An initial goal of
20 million trees was surpassed and in the yearly time frame the company
planted nearly 22 million new coffee seedlings resistant to leaf rust.

Today, 40 million coffee trees have been donated to farmers in Mexico,
Guatemala, and El Salvador. The vision has been extended by Starbucks,
and the company plans to have 100 million healthy coffee trees to farmers
by 2025. The Starbucks Global Impact Report 2019 announced, "As of
June 2020, the next 10 million are being distributed, with close monitor-
ing of potential complications related to COVID-19." The Plant a Tree

program helps farmers and their families, Starbucks, and the coffee industry, assisting quality arabica coffee to sustain and be available in the future.

Global Farmer Fund

Starbucks began investing in farmer loans in 2000, helping farmer cooperatives to strengthen and expand their business with reasonable credit terms. Coffee farmers are often viewed as risky loan recipients making it challenging for hard-working growers to obtain any form of financing. Today, the investments with loan partners such as Root Capital, who supplies agricultural businesses with capital and training to help them grow, and Fair Trade Access Fund address the long-term needs of the smallholder farmer in developing countries; medium-term and long-term financing options have become available. The cooperatives receive not only financial assistance but education in agronomy and business practices. According to the company, loan partners have made loans in thirteen countries, including "Peru, Nicaragua, Honduras, Rwanda, Guatemala, Mexico, Costa Rica, Colombia, Kenya, Uganda, The Democratic Republic of Congo, Tanzania and Indonesia." Not only does this increase the profitability of the famer but also works to strengthen the coffee quality. As of June 2020, Starbucks Global Farmer Loan Fund had allocated $49 million in farmer loans and is set to meet its commitment to distribute $50 million in farmer loans worldwide by 2020.

Support in Emergencies

Starbucks Emergency Relief Fund is aimed at the most vulnerable farming communities. In late 2018, coffee prices in Central America had plummeted to low levels, impacted by bumper coffee crops in Brazil and Vietnam. Plentiful supplies from the strong crops forced coffee prices to lower internationally. Farmers in Central America struggled just to cover production and labor costs, much less make a profit. As an action plan, considering the company's commitment to make coffee economically sustainable, Starbucks committed to assist small farmers with whom the company does business. The funds were targeted to farmers in Mexico, Guatemala, Nicaragua, and El Salvador and used to subsidize farmer income during the upcoming harvest season. In fiscal 2019, Starbucks paid $20 million to over 8,000 farmers. Today, the coffee market prices have rebounded over the cost of production, but Starbucks has again proven it stands ready to support the coffee farmer.

Origin Grants

Starbucks helps the farming family by creating opportunities for women. The company believes an investment in women will have a beneficial impact for the farming community as a whole. On International Women's Day, March 8, 2018, the Starbucks Foundation announced a goal of empowering 250,000 women in origin communities by 2025. To date, over 66,000 women have been positively impacted through programs on leadership skills, access to finance, and healthier homes (see Table 4.2 for

Table 4.2 Current Origin Grant Recipients

(Organization/Project Location/Purpose)

Lutheran World Relief

Project Location: Columbia and Indonesia

Purpose: Empower women through increased sanitation and greater economic opportunity, e.g., promoting women's leadership in cooperatives through gender-integration training.

Days for Girls

Project Location: Rwanda

Purpose: Provide low-income women farmers with menstrual supplies, community health education, and entrepreneurial opportunities.

Grounds for Health

Project Location: Ethiopia

Purpose: Ensure the health and well-being of women in coffee-growing communities through cervical care cancer prevention and treatment.

Send a Cow

Project Location: Rwanda

Purpose: Equip women with the skill and confidence to get the most productivity from their farmland.

World Neighbors

Project Location: Guatemala

Purpose: Furnish women with the skills and education to start and run a system and savings and credit groups, thus aiding community entrepreneurship.

World Relief

Project Location: Rwanda

Purpose: Teach women to prosper through safe relationships, healthy homes, clean drinking water, and the formation of savings groups.

Source: Starbucks Coffee Company, *Investing in Coffee Communities*, www.starbucks.com

grants, locations, and purpose). Women from coffee- and tea-growing communities across Africa, Asia, and Latin America have benefited from the opportunities which were developed through eighteen grants, totaling more than $5 million.

Starbucks Partners to Aid Columbian Coffee Farmers

Columbia is the second largest producer of arabica coffee behind Brazil, and Starbucks is its largest buyer for the country. Coffee farmers in Columbia have faced numerous challenges during the country's fifty-year-plus civil war conflict (1964–2016). In 2016, a historic peace treaty was signed between Columbia's government and the Revolutionary Armed Forces of Columbia that ended the decades-long armed conflict. It has been a struggle for many farmers to maintain their crops, some even unable to reach their land high in the mountains due to blocked areas during the civil unrest.

It is commonplace for the company to collaborate with other agencies, and Starbucks showed its support to the Columbian coffee farmers in a number of ways: in 2012, opening a Farmer Support Center in Manizales to connect farmers with training and education; in 2013, partnering with U.S. Agency for International Development (USAID) on a soil analysis program; in 2014, expanding the USAID program to aid young coffee farmers in post-conflict areas; and in 2017, partnering with the Inter-American Developmental Bank (IDB) on a loan initiative directed toward women-led coffee growers.

USAID "leads international development and humanitarian efforts to save lives, reduce poverty, strengthen democratic governance and help people progress beyond assistance" and was a strong collaborative partner for Starbucks. Starbucks invested $1.5 million in the program, which was matched with $1.5 million by the government agency, in order to focus on the quality of coffee crops. Soil samples were taken and analyzed, often cost prohibitive for farmers, in order to address deficiencies in the soil. Ultimately, 25,000 coffee farmers benefited from this program.

In a news release (*Starbucks Stories.* "Starbucks Invests in the Next Generation of Columbian Coffee Farmers." Starbucks Coffee Company, July 10, 2017), the company detailed the extension of the USAID participation in the program the following year with an additional $519,000, focusing on youth and technology:

> Engaging 1,000 young coffee farmers in the country's post-conflict zones across Cauca and Tolima.
>
> Offering technical assistance, agricultural training, and access to improved technologies such as laptops to help run their businesses.

The development of three native tree nurseries, benefiting at least 150 coffee farmers and indirectly about 1,000 people in communities across Caldas, Huila, and Cauca, through reforestation and climate resiliency programs.

The IDB is the "leading source of development financing for Latin America and the Caribbean" and a partner with Starbucks in its efforts to aid Columbian farmers. Starbucks is pairing with IDB in a $4 million project to support 2,000 women-led growers in the Columbian states of Antioquia and Chocó. A total of $2 million of the funding will come from Starbucks Global Farmer Loan Fund and up to $2 million will be provided via the IDB through its Multilateral Investment Fund.

The program, aimed at financing opportunities, is described by the company in press documents (*Starbucks Stories.* "Starbucks Invests in the Next Generation of Columbian Coffee Farmers." Starbucks Coffee Company, July 10, 2017) to include the following specifics:

A system for the members of the Cooperandes co-op, most whom are women, to access financing needed to enhance coffee yields and quality among member producers.

An opportunity to provide short and long term assistance through a unique financing model that provides low-risk loans to farmers for renovation, with complementary technical assistance being provided.

This innovative approach to financing brings together multiple actors within the supply chain from the supplier (COEX), the cooperative (Cooperandes) and Starbucks, who not only provides counterpart financing for the loan, but will also guarantee market access for the loan recipients, through its C.A.F.E. Practices methodology.

By helping coffee farming families, young farmers, and women, the company is aiming to sustain the Columbia coffee community. Columbian coffee is beloved around the globe and certainly by Starbucks customers. Check out one of the Columbia Reserve small-lot coffees, the single-origin Columbia Coffee described as "balanced and nutty" or the Columbia Nariño Espresso described as "elegant and layered."

Did You Know?

According to Starbucks Coffee Company's *Nutrition by the Cup*, based on the company's standard brewing methods, an espresso contains 75 milligrams of caffeine per shot (1 fluid ounce), and brewed coffee contains 20 milligrams of caffeine per fluid ounce.

Sustainable Future

Starbucks is not alone in its commitment to make coffee the world's first sustainably sourced agricultural product. Starbucks has high aspirations and is doing its part to build a sustainable future for coffee and ensuring the supply of coffee for future generations. The company is a member of the Sustainable Coffee Challenge, a movement of more than 135 members striving toward this goal. While an industry leader at 99 percent ethically sourced coffee, the company continues to reach for 100 percent ethically sourced coffee. Starbucks has invested in agronomy research and development, Farmer Support Centers, and Emergency Relief Funds; partnered with government agencies; provided farmer financing and education; planted rust-resistant trees; and created opportunities for women in coffee communities, and ethical sourcing. The company is keenly aware that coffee farming must be successful for coffee to be sustainable.

Coffee Master Program

Starbucks understands the importance of education and putting its partners' knowledge to productive use. The Starbucks Coffee Master program was initiated in 2004, and over a decade later the company reported that there were more than 5,000 active Starbucks Coffee Masters around the globe. In the program, partners receive education in coffee brewing, tasting, and blends. An individual behind the Starbucks counter in a black apron, instead of green, signals that the partner has been awarded the certification of Coffee Master. A Coffee Master has been through a special program to learn about the growing and roasting aspects of the industry. The history of coffee along with coffee crafting and demonstrations is also included. It is not an easy feat; partners must pass a series of tests following their training before they are named Coffee Masters. Many of the personnel at Starbucks headquarters in Seattle are Coffee Masters, too.

The education proponent has been a win–win for partners, customers, and Starbucks. Partners gain knowledge of coffee and the industry and a further fondness for the craft. Customers gain from their expertise and can ask the resident Coffee Master any questions they have about coffee. The program encourages partners to enter into dialogue with Starbucks customers and share their further coffee knowledge. Starbucks wins because happy partners and customers are both good for business.

Starbucks Global Coffee Academy

Launched in 2017, Starbucks Global Academy (SGA) is a global platform created in partnership with Arizona State University for Starbucks partners, customers, and community members. It is free of charge to anyone interested in learning by simply registering online at the website https://www.starbucksglobalacademy.com/. The courses on SGA are "designed to improve careers and strengthen communities." Those interested in increasing their personal knowledge or professional skills have over eighty courses to choose from in a host of educational fields. Learning is online, convenient, and self-paced with modules, readings, videos, and review questions. Career classes include such courses as Business Leadership Design: Speaking the Language of Your Customer, Leveraging Your Network, and How to See Problems as Opportunities. Personal enrichment courses include Happiness and Well-Being, Programming for Everyone: Introduction to Programming, and Community Connectedness.

For individuals working in the coffee field or for those simply interested in the coffee culture, the educational platform provides timely study. Three additional platforms are available on SGA: Greener Apron, To Be Welcoming, and Coffee Academy. The Greener Apron course is open to all, not just Starbucks partners, to learn about sustainability and what it really means at Starbucks. To Be Welcoming is a project that explores bias through a fifteen-course curriculum, designed in concert with Arizona State University to address bias through understanding the human experience. As the SGA website explains, "Public spaces and third places are more welcoming to all when we celebrate our shared humanity." A new Coffee Academy consists of five in-depth classes which allow you to learn about coffee as a crop, roasting, blending, ethical sourcing, and beverage crafting. Starbucks supports the coffee community through education, allowing partners, customers, and community members to share their knowledge and expose others to the world of coffee and sustainability.

Coffee Niche

Customers can further refine their favorite coffee niche by deciding if they favor light, medium, or dark roasts. Starbucks was founded on a medium and dark-roast coffee, but in 2012 the company introduced Starbucks® Blonde Roast, a lighter roast. For many the taste of Starbucks was considered too harsh. This roast is a lighter-bodied coffee and may have great appeal to a new coffee consumer because it has a mild taste and gentle finish. Blonde, also known as light, has a shorter roasting time, which retains more of the original flavors. The company has other coffees available in the Blonde selection; lighter roasts are more acidic and known for floral aromas.

For those new to coffee drinking and not sure of their preferred roast, the company has a quiz which coffee consumers can take online. On the company's website https://www.starbucks.com/coffee, the Starbucks Coffee Finder has been prepared with the help of Starbucks coffee masters. The coffee investigation takes a few brief moments, and upon completion of responses to several simple questions Starbucks will provide recommendations of coffees in the suggested roast spectrum. The survey begins with a descriptive query, "How would you describe yourself?" Quiz-takers may pick Lighthearted & Sunny, Balanced & Easy-Going, or Bold & Complex. A fun quick quiz, the company will "match you with the coffee that suits you best."

Medium roast is in the middle of the spectrum and roasts for a shorter time than the dark roast, allowing the flavor of the bean to pop. Roasting to the mid-level becomes slightly darker than the light roast. Medium roasts have a sweetness, and many of the unique flavors of the coffee's origin tend to remain. The company describes its medium roast as "Medium-roasted coffee beans are smooth and balanced, with rich, approachable flavors." A dark roast is the most aromatic, with low acidity and chocolate and caramel notes. The company describes its dark roast, "Dark-roasted coffees have fuller body with robust, bold taste."

Starbucks carries over thirty varieties of blends and single-origination coffees. Among the handcrafted beverages the store features are fresh-brewed coffees, hot and iced espresso beverages, coffee and noncoffee blended beverages, hot chocolates, and teas. Each of Starbucks' thirty-plus coffees has a distinctive flavor. This is just one of the ways the company has moved ahead of its competition—by having a flavor that's appealing to everyone. You can tell a lot about each coffee according to where it was grown. There are three growing regions that represent the source of all arabica coffee beans, and coffee from each region has a distinct flavor, unique to the area where it originates.

Starbucks has specific coffees from different countries, and each of these coffees has unique flavor characteristics. These are referred to within the company as single-origin coffees. Blends, on the other hand, bring together coffees from different areas, or origins, to create a different taste experience. Some coffees are purchased solely for blending, while others are purchased as single-origin offerings. Blending permits some unique taste variations.

Coffees from Latin America typically carry the flavors of soft spice, nuts, and cocoa. Central and South America top world coffee production;

they produce more than any other growing region. These coffees have consistent quality and are fabulous for blending. Starbucks typically sources from the countries of Brazil, Colombia, Costa Rica, El Salvador, Guatemala, Honduras, Nicaragua, Mexico, Panama, Peru, and Puerto Rico. One example of a single-origin coffee is Guatemala Antigua. This coffee, with a slightly nutty taste, comes from the Antigua Valley with hints of chocolate and caramel.

Coffees from the Africa and Arabia region are known for their berry-like and citrusy flavors. Favorites in this area include coffees from Ethiopia, Kenya, Rwanda, and Tanzania. An example from this region is from the limited time only, single-origin collection, Sun Dried Ethiopian Sidamo Coffee. This coffee, celebrating the birthplace of arabica coffee, is definitely fruity flavored with black cherry flavors and chocolate notes.

Coffees from the Asia and Pacific region are bold, with earthy, herbal, or spicy flavors. An example is Decaf Sumatra Coffee. Sumatra, by the way, is the sixth largest island in the world and is home to Mount Kerinci, a 12,467-foot peak. Decaf Sumatra may be a decaffeinated coffee, but it has an intense flavor, with an earthy undertone.

The company is also well known for its blended coffees, a mixture of two or more origin coffee beans. A new favorite introduced in 2019 is Siren's Blend, a flavorful blend of medium roast whole-bean coffee. "The juicy, citrusy and chocolaty blend combines coffee from East Africa and Latin America. Named for the Siren that symbolizes Starbucks, this blend honors the innovations of women, from farmer to roaster to barista." A portion of the sales from this popular blend help support women in the coffee origin communities.

Beverage Terminology

According to Economic Research Service Food Availability Data from the USDA, a reduction in regular coffee consumption in the United States has transpired over the past seventy years. Annual U.S. coffee consumption is less than half of what it was at its peak in 1946, at 46.42 gallons per person; compare that to 20 gallons per person in 2015. Why? Possibly because other options, such as soft drinks and a host of nontraditional coffee options—chilled cappuccinos, espressos, lattes—have permeated the coffee culture.

A review of the basic types of specialty coffee drinks follows. Coffee creations can be complicated, and Starbucks puts a unique spin on each, along with a host of additional options.

Americano: A style of coffee made by combining hot water with espresso. The strength of an Americano can vary depending on the amount of water and the amount of espresso added.

Cappuccino: A beverage made from espresso, hot steamed milk, and frothed milk.

Espresso: A strong, concentrated coffee made by forcing hot water through finely ground coffee beans under pressure.

Flat White: A coffee beverage made with espresso, topped with a very small or thin, flat layer of steamed milk. Consequently, a flat white has a stronger taste than a latte as it carries a higher ratio of espresso to steamed milk.

Latte: A coffee beverage made with espresso and topped with steamed milk. Often, the ratio is one-third espresso topped with two-thirds steamed milk.

Macchiato: Means marked in Italian, and an espresso macchiato is espresso marked with a small amount of foamed milk.

Mocha: A type of high-quality coffee bean from Arabia. This term also describes a beverage combining chocolate and a form of coffee, usually espresso.

Size Selection

Think about the last time you went into a restaurant or a coffeehouse and ordered a drink. You might have ordered an extra large if you were super thirsty or wanted to savor a nice, hot beverage that would last awhile. A little java or just something quick to quench your thirst might have called for a small. Starbucks is definitely a trendy café, and it operates a cut above the mega fast-food establishments. Case in point—its cup sizes for hot and cold beverages. Hot beverages range from Short (8 fluid ounces) to Tall (12 fluid ounces), Grande (16 fluid ounces), and Venti (20 fluid ounces). Cold beverages range from Tall (12 fluid ounces) to Grande (16 fluid ounces) to Venti (24 fluid ounces) and Trenta (31 fluid ounces). So you can go into a competitor and ask for a small coffee, or you can go into Starbucks and ask for a tall. You'd be served a 12-ounce cup in either place, but doesn't a *tall* sound so much more impressive?

Did You Know?

According to the Specialty Coffee Association, it takes about forty-two coffee beans to make an average serving of espresso.

Brewing Methodologies

Coffee from across the globe, perhaps whole-bean Starbucks coffee from Ethiopia or a tasty ground blend from Columbia, can be served at home. The long journey from the farming field to the kitchen provides an opportunity to sample and enjoy the bean taste from various regions. Coffee drinkers can experiment with the roast spectrum, blends, and origin coffees to find their niche.

It is easy to obtain a properly brewed cup of coffee at Starbucks or other coffeehouses, but how do you make the same high quality of coffee at home? Preground is ready to go but for those who have whole beans and you need a coffee grinder, typically it is a matter of experimentation to obtain your preferred consistency. If whole beans are used, coffee should be ground each time a pot of coffee is prepared.

The recommended size of the coffee grind depends on the brew methodology. For a short brew time, the grind should be finer, and for longer brew times, coarser. Fine grinds of coffee have a powdery texture and flavor can be extracted quickly. Coarse coffee beans have been through minimal grinding and large parts of the coffee beans remain, recommended for a slow extraction of flavor. The coarse coffee bean is often described as chunky and similar in size to sea salt. A medium grind, akin to the size of table salt, is a common grind for most preground coffee packages. Although there are many methods for brewing coffee, a drip coffee machine, pour over, French press, and a siphon brewer are four popular methods one can utilize at home.

Drip Coffee Machine: A convenient, quick, and easy means for making coffee is a coffee maker. A proper balance of water and coffee makes a savory cup, and Starbucks recommends abiding by the general rule of thumb, two tablespoons of ground coffee for each six ounces of water. Machine style and design is a matter of individual taste preference and there are a multitude of options, but the filter basket will be either a cone-shaped or a flat-bottom filter. Cone-shaped filters have a design which enhances the flow of water so finely ground coffee is typically recommended. With a flat-bottom filter, coffee grinds will be immersed in water longer so typically a medium grind is preferred.

Pour-Over Method: Hot water is poured over finely ground coffee in a paper filter, in a slow and steady motion, and the water passes through the filter into a coffee cup. Coffee aficionados typically premoisten the filter to eliminate any flavors from the filter that may transfer to the coffee. This is a compelling method for many because it is a simple manual process and does not require an investment in expensive equipment.

A short process to obtain the brew, roughly just 3 minutes from the time of pouring, is best for light roasts, where the beans have more contact with the water which will bring out the original flavor and floral aroma.

French Press: Many terms are used to describe this plunger method for brewing coffee: Coffee Press, Press Pot, and even Plunger Coffee. Whatever description is used, the French Press makes a full-bodied, strong cup of coffee and is often the preferred method of coffee connoisseurs. The French Press is a manual coffee maker with a straightforward preparation. The French Press should be filled with hot water and ground coffee beans, stirred, and brewed for 4 minutes. The plunger should slowly be pressed down to the bottom of the pot in order to filter the coffee grounds. The grind should be coarse so it is unable to pass through the filter and can obtain the full, rich flavor of the bean.

Siphon Brewer: Sometimes referred to as a vac pot, a siphon brewer is a beautiful, artful way to prepare coffee. A catchy design, a plus of a siphon brewer is that two chambers are utilized to brew coffee where vacuum pressure is used to produce coffee. Coffee prepared by a siphon brewer, a roughly 10-minute process, is recommended with a medium grind and commonly described as clean and light flavored.

Coffee should be stored in an airtight container and left at room temperature. A pantry or kitchen cabinet is often the best option, even on the kitchen counter, if it is not exposed to heat. Storing in the refrigerator or freezer is not recommended due to moisture forming from condensation. According to an April 2012 Starbucks news release, *Fact Sheet: Four Fundamentals of Brewing,* the company explains, "Coffee's biggest enemies are oxygen and moisture," words for coffee lovers to take to heart.

CHAPTER FIVE

Digital Innovation and Technology

For me, the status quo could not stand. We had to elevate backroom and customer-facing technology to a more strategic, proactive level, a shift that had to begin at the top of the organization.
—Howard Schultz, Chairman Emeritus Starbucks,
Onward: How Starbucks Fought for Its Life without Losing Its Soul (2011)

Digital innovation is often referred to simply as a new idea or method or the development of a new or redesigned good or service achieved by utilizing digital tools. Technology is the knowledge or techniques devoted to designing and producing goods and services. Rapidly advancing technology is the key to supporting digital innovation. Whether it is a lab for project testing, a consumer-friendly mobile app, a rapidly expanding delivery system, team-inspired digital music, or clutter-free wireless charging, Starbucks knows customers want new and heightened products and services. Read on to see how Starbucks sustains the cutting edge of technological advancement and innovative thought.

Social Media by the Numbers

Starbucks social media team is top notch, beginning with an intriguing and up-to-date website ranked in the 2018 Best Global Websites (#22) by Byte Level Research. Through the years the company has also built an engaged online community, evidenced by the substantial follower count:

Facebook: 35,604,788 million followers

YouTube: 309,000 subscribers
Twitter: 10.9 million followers
Pinterest: 431,350 followers
Instagram: 18.1 million followers

Source data: Numbers as of January 25, 2021.

Starbucks Lab

Advancing innovation, Starbucks opened its own lab in November 2018. The 20,000-square-foot lab, dubbed the Tryer Center, is located on the ground floor of the company's Seattle headquarters. The catchy name "Tryer" is actually a coffee term. A tryer is located on the drum roaster and is a tool used to capture a sample of coffee during the roasting process. Fast-paced innovation is paramount in the lab—hundred days or less, to be exact. According to CEO Kevin Johnson in Starbucks Stories, dated June 11, 2019, "We've gone from a long-cycle approach to innovation, to one where we try to go from idea to action in 100 days, and we learn and adapt along the way."

At the time of the news release, more than 130 projects had been developed and tested at the lab, with many making it into stores. There have been failures as well as successes. Starbucks soup and soup-warming equipment was a no-go, but the Cloud Macchiato, the company's widely successful drink, was tested in the lab with good results before it was launched nationally in early March 2019. If you are envisioning your high school science lab, think much bigger. The company describes the lab—with its 3D printer, prototype sketches, and neon signs—as looking like a cross between a laboratory, a design firm, and a dot-com start-up. Think mock stores, movable walls, trendy tasting centers and testing centers, and a mock drive-up station.

The new project ideas are generated by Starbucks partners, with the Tryer Center in service to make the lives of partners and customers better. Along with technical innovations, such as the Precision Milk Dispenser Machine, watch for drinks coming from Cold Pop, a small store inside the Tryer Center. Open three days a week, Cold Pop serves 200 drinks per day to partners at $5 a beverage. Employees taste and then chime in on potential concoctions, and the funds generated go to a good cause—The Cup Fund—benefitting partners in financial need.

Starbucks Mobile App

The Starbucks green siren logo is a widely utilized app built on personalization. Launched in 2009, today's app is very customer friendly. You can place an order for drinks and food via the app, personalize your order, and go straight to the pick-up counter for your treat. No more waiting in line. On the app, you will be asked to confirm your store and then pay for your order with a previously loaded Starbucks card—all very fast and efficient. The app even remembers your customizations for your drink.

Additionally, you can send gift cards to friends and family members via the app. This may come in handy for your holiday shopping. A bit of Starbucks trivia: Over the last few years, one in six Americans received a Starbucks gift card for Christmas. The store recently added a host of enhancements to its Rewards loyalty program, experiencing exceptional growth during COVID-19 with modified store operations. For fiscal 2020, U.S. Reward members grew 10 percent to 19.3 million while China Reward members grew 34 percent to 13.5 million members. Customers who use a registered Starbucks card for purchases can earn freebies galore by accumulating reward point "Stars."

Order Your Starbucks Drink with a Voice Command

Let's say you are cleaning the kitchen, doing intermittent leg squats, and watching your favorite TV program, all at once. Now you want to order your Starbucks beverage in order to have a delicious treat for your upcoming morning meeting. Clearly you are a multitasker, and Google Assistant may be a great problem solver for your busy lifestyle. You will need to take a few minutes to download the Google Assistant app and pair it to your Starbucks Reward account. A few minutes of prep time will be well worth the effort, as a simple voice command, "Order Starbucks," is all it takes. Just hit the audio microphone (or type if you wish) and order away. You will have a pleasant interactive conversation with the Assistant. Be mindful, if your order is very complex, you may need to try a few times to get it right. Once complete, you will need to give the Assistant permission to access your location in order to find the closest Starbucks, then confirm the payment information, and off you go! Your beverage will be waiting, and you can be on your way to the meeting in minutes.

Music

Music has long been a part of the history of Starbucks, beginning with a dedicated entertainment team in 1994 selecting original CDs. Today, music is still at the heart of the coffeehouse, but its entertainment is all high tech. In 2016, Starbucks launched a digital music experience with Spotify, a leading music podcast and video-streaming service. The team now chooses the artists and songs, along with special guest DJ pop-ups, which are available on Starbucks playlists on Spotify.

Starbucks app users can now immediately discover music playing overhead in stores, save Starbucks songs to a playlist on Spotify, and listen to the music on Spotify anywhere they go. In a Starbucks Stories press release, dated January 19, 2016, Howard Schultz noted:

> Today is the next era in that experience. We are merging the physical and digital, providing new access points for Spotify as they continue to grow globally, placing more control into our customers' hands and giving artists the world's largest stage for them to share their talent.

The mobile app customers can always find the Starbucks music playlist on the app by looking for the musical icon. Starbucks public playlists are available on Spotify to anyone with a Spotify account. If a barista would like to change the store's music, Spotify provides a tool so they can choose from a multitude of Starbucks playlists, updated weekly, to fit the vibe of their store. Baristas get a complimentary premium Spotify account.

The Seattle Cashless Store Experiment

An increasing number of retail stores and service companies have entered the cashless society. This means a store will accept credit cards, debit cards, or payment via an app, but no cash. Uber, Mexican restaurant Dos Toros, and the Tampa Bay Rays at Tropicana Field are all examples of cashless retail environments.

Why would an establishment not want to accept dollars? Cards do have certain benefits over cash. Cards are a fast-paced means for payment—insert card and you are done. It is quicker to move through a retail payment line with a card versus cash. Cash is clumsy; it takes time to pull it out of a wallet, it must be counted by the attendant, and possibly change needs to be given back. Customers move through the payment line at a faster pace with a card. Cash is also an open target for dishonest employees. If you have a cashless store, there is less temptation for a robbery because thieves would rather prey on cash-based businesses.

A technological innovation, Starbucks tested out a cashless store by starting a trial run in early 2018 at the busy downtown Seattle location in Russell Investments Center. Credit, debit, or mobile app payments were accepted. Rather than posting signs, baristas politely informed customers they were not accepting cash. Apparently, the customers did not mind because the experiment turned into practice. As of 2019, a barista from the Seattle store said her location had been a no-cash store for a little over a year and doing quite well.

While there are certain advantages to the no-cash store, not everyone is a fan. Some say a cashless store is a form of discrimination. Lower-income individuals or people with volatile employment are less likely to have a checking or savings account and less likely to have either a debit or credit card. The wave of cashless retailers has caused much discussion and even legal rulings. Massachusetts has had a law since 1978 that stores in the state must accept cash, and New Jersey recently imposed a similar rule. In 2019, Philadelphia became the first city to require retailers to accept cash, with legislation pending in some other major cities. So, does it look like all U.S. Starbucks stores will be going cashless anytime soon? Probably not. Even in a tech-oriented economy, cash still plays a major role.

Tech Trivia

1. There are 19.3 million Starbucks Rewards Members, driving 47 percent of the company sales in the United States in the last two quarters of 2020.
2. Starbucks has delivery service in more than fifteen countries, including Canada, China, Japan, the United Kingdom, and Mexico.
3. In 2018, Starbucks set up its first virtual store in China with the aid of Alibaba's technology and Starbucks Delivers.
4. Technology strategies and innovations are so vital to the company that Starbucks has its own Chief Technology Officer, Gerri Martin-Flickinger, who also serves as an executive vice president.
5. Starbucks invested $100 million in a new fund, Valor Siren Ventures I L.P., which will support start-up firms developing technologies and solutions for the food and retail industry.
6. In Robeson, North Carolina, the company owns a 140,000-panel solar farm, delivering enough energy to power the equivalent of 600 Starbucks stores in North Carolina, Virginia, Delaware, Kentucky, Maryland, West Virginia, and D.C.

7. The company invited customers who wished to support the relief efforts after Hurricane Florence to donate to the American Red Cross via the Starbucks mobile app.
8. Technology was front and center at the Starbucks annual meeting on March 20, 2019, at WaMu Theater in downtown Seattle, with "43 monitors, dozens of computers, three cameras, and miles of cable to power the auditorium's 12 displays, including the 66-foot screen onstage."
9. Starbucks delivered 22,709 iPads to 8,500 stores for use in their May 29, 2018 antibias training.
10. In 2009, Starbucks began offering complimentary Wi-Fi at its stores.

Source: Starbucks Corporation.

Wireless Charging Stations

Starbucks anticipates and plans for customer needs, and with wireless charging stations in stores, customers don't need to search for an old-fashioned plug-in station or a scarce electrical outlet. In 2012, Starbucks and Powermat, now the largest wireless charging network in the world, began a pilot program at select stores in the Boston area, equipping the stores with wireless charging. The pilot program was clearly a hit with customers and was quickly expanded. In 2014, Starbucks announced a national rollout of wireless charging spots, beginning with stores in San Francisco, with a full rollout to Starbucks company-operated stores over time.

Equipped stores have wireless charging spots where you place your phone to charge while enjoying your coffee. This is clutter-free and sleek, as no cords or wires are required. If your phone does not have embedded wireless charging, you can use a ring adapter. Techy alert—the Powermat uses an inductive charging method using an electromagnetic field to transfer energy rather than electrical currents to charge your phone. Wireless charging spots are widely available now. How do you know if your Starbucks has wireless charging? Log on to your computer and visit powermat.com/locations to check out the ever-growing locales. You will find locations which may be helpful to you when traveling or you find yourself without a charge. Better yet, for those on the go, be sure to download the Powermat app.

Delivery

Along with the convenience of the Starbucks mobile app, customers can now order a select Starbucks menu and have the coffee and food delivered to their home or office. After a successful initial pilot program in Miami in the fall of 2018, "Starbucks Delivers" moved ahead with gusto. The test saw positive feedback and exhibited strong demand, so in early 2019 the company announced expansion of the program in the United States. Starbucks Delivers is available in twelve countries currently. The company is in partnership with Uber Eats, an online food ordering and delivery platform, and is currently available across the United States including Miami. The cities are Seattle, the Bay area, Los Angeles, Chicago, Boston, New York, and D.C.

While customers use the Starbucks app to order ahead and pay when they are picking up their own food and drink, at the time of this writing, customers must use the Uber Eats app to place orders for delivery. If coffee customers want to find out whether Starbucks delivers in their hometown, they just have to check out the listing of current Starbucks stores on Uber Eats: https://www.ubereats.com.

For those who can't order Starbucks through Uber Eats, other food delivery options are available. In 2015, the company teamed up with Postmates, online delivery for restaurants, retailers, grocery, and convenience stores, for delivery in Seattle. The delivery area has grown, and to find out if your area Starbucks is served by Postmates, check out www.postmates.com for a list of current locations. Select stores offer Starbucks delivery through DoorDash, an on-demand restaurant delivery system. You can check out local Starbucks deliveries from DoorDash, and be sure to check frequently as DoorDash cities are expanding quickly.

Delivery is not just to your house or office; curbside delivery is another channel of convenience the company is enhancing. In 2020, the company launched Curbside Pick Up in over 800 U.S. company-operated stores. Curbside Pick Up became a popular method during the COVID-19 pandemic and one which Starbucks is continuing to enhance. By the end of fiscal 2021, the company plans to have this delivery methodology available in roughly 2,000 stores across the United States.

Blockchain Technology

You likely have heard the term "blockchain" at work or browsing through a computer magazine, but what does it mean? Blockchain technology is real-time information, continuously updated, and shared with all users. Starbucks refers to it as "traceable technology," saying it will aid in the bean-to-cup traceability, essentially for the farmers' financial empowerment. In 2018, Starbucks launched a pilot program with select coffee farmers in Costa Rica, Columbia, and Rwanda to share real-time information of the journey of the coffee bean in a ledger. The pilot program is essential because it explores the viability of utilizing the traceability feature with the company's 400,000-plus farmers. The purpose of the program is to positively impact everyone within the supply chain, and Starbucks is using the Microsoft Azure Blockchain platform to track this activity.

At the 2019 Starbucks annual meeting, Senior Vice President, Global Coffee & Tea, Michelle Burns previewed a digital traceability feature that was being tested for possible inclusion within the app. Customers can digitally scan and trace a package of coffee, see where it was grown and roasted, and watch its journey from farm to customer. The following year, in 2020, the traceability feature became a reality, not only within the app but customers can now utilize their laptop to trace their favorite coffee at traceability.starbucks.com. The people who grow the coffee can be connected with the people who drink the coffee. For customers interested in knowing more about their coffee origins and the farmers who grow their favorite brand, this is transparency at its finest. Customers can see first-hand the farmers they are supporting with their coffee purchase. Farmers, too, will know where their coffee beans are going and perhaps enjoy a bit of fame and notoriety.

Did You Know?

Your cup of joe is 98 percent water so the type of water used for brew will certainly impact the taste. The water source should be clear, should be free of impurities, and have no odor. Consider using one of the many commercially made water filters to remove impurities if tap water is not ideal in order to fulfill the quest for the perfect-tasting cup of coffee.

Data Analytics Assist in Store Placement

Have you ever wondered how Starbucks decides where to place their next new store? Is it because of good vibes, a premonition, or technology? Of course, if you guessed technology, you would be correct. And while actual partners at Starbucks make the final decision on where to open new stores, the data platform is the force behind pinpointing these sites. Through the company Esri, a global market leader in geographic information systems (GIS), Starbucks has superior data assistance guiding the company on the best places to open stores in the United States and worldwide. In case you have not heard of a GIS, it is defined as a computer program designed to capture, analyze, manage, and interpret geographic information.

One of the major uses for this data assistance prepared for Starbucks, dubbed Atlas, is to assist with the complex problem of store location. The information provided by Atlas is highly detailed, taking into account such details as new office construction, retail clusters, trade areas, traffic patterns, demographics, and new location decisions on existing stores. A special behind-the-scenes peek of how GIS works at Starbucks was provided at the 2014 Esri User Conference in a presentation entitled "Starbucks Coffee and IT Starbucks." Lawrence North, Director of Business Intelligence Strategy and Solutions, describes the system: "It's a large GIS application that includes workflow, analysis and store performance." North noted the application has been, and continues to be, an incredible success story for Starbucks. Patrick O'Hagan, Director of Market Planning, notes that once a location has been decided upon, Atlas will take you through "approval, permitting, construction and eventually opening." It is one-stop shopping for store placement. (Intrigued? Check out the video entitled "ESRI 2014 UC: Starbucks Coffee and IT" on Esri's website at https://www.esri.com/videos)

Annual Shareholder's Meeting

In the ultimate nod to technological innovation, the Starbucks Annual Meeting of Shareholders on March 18, 2020, was held virtually. The shareholders' meeting, previously held at the WaMu Theater in downtown Seattle, is typically a widely anticipated celebration and social event. Due to COVID-19 health concerns, the company quickly transitioned to a virtual format. In addition to the quick store modifications for drive-thru service, increased delivery, adjusted store hours, and closures, the annual get-together saw changes, too.

While the Starbucks board of directors were present, technology allowed for all to join virtually. The virtual meeting format was jam-packed with video presentations, background music, and a question-and-answer session with management. The twenty-eighth meeting of shareholders lasted just under an hour with a notably different agenda, as noted by Kevin Johnson, seated at the Starbucks Support Center in Seattle. While conducting official business that normally transpires during an annual meeting, such as voting for the board of directors by stockholders (done via a polling process), the focus was on the navigation of COVID-19 safety measures in their stores around the world. Johnson highlighted the company's three priorities: the health and well-being of partners, partnering with local health officials and governments, and Starbucks showing up as a positive member of each of its 32,000-plus communities. He stressed, "We prioritize these three principles over everything else, including any near-term economic implications."

CHAPTER SIX

Social Impact

Early on at Starbucks, we quickly figured out that when there was pain—economic pain, conflict, or disappointment over a failed idea—our hat was still our hat, our values were still our values, and sticking with them was the most important thing we could do.

—Howard Behar, former president, Starbucks
International, *It's Not about the Coffee: Leadership
Principles from a Life at Starbucks* (2007)

The Starbucks Experience

Going to Starbucks is a unique experience, a Third Place between work and home where customers can find superior coffee and a place to relax or socialize with friends. The Starbucks experience is referenced in press releases and Starbucks literature. On the Starbucks website, the About Us section explains, "It's just a moment in time—just one hand reaching over the counter to present a cup to another outstretched hand. But it's a connection. We make sure everything we do honors that connection—from our commitment to the highest quality coffee in the world, to the way we engage with our customers and communities and to do business responsibly." Memos from former leader Howard Schultz and current head, Kevin Johnson, constantly extol the virtues of the Starbucks experience. It permeates the culture of the company. In fact, the mission of the coffeehouse reads, "To inspire and nurture the human spirit—one person, one cup and one neighborhood at a time."

One thing is clear—it *is* all about the customer. Starbucks combines quality products with building a personal relationship with each customer. Schultz explains, "At Starbucks, our product is not just great coffee but also what we call the 'Starbucks experience': an inviting, enriching environment in our stores that is comfortable and accessible, yet also stylish and elegant" (Schultz and Yang 1997, 251). As of fiscal year-end 2020, roughly 349,000 employees were bringing the Starbucks experience to life in over 32,000 stores worldwide. The company strives to build a personal relationship with each of its customers.

According to the 2018 Annual Report, "The Starbucks Experience is built upon superior customer service and a seamless digital experience as well as clean and well-maintained stores that reflect the personalities of the communities in which they operate, thereby building a high degree of customer loyalty." Starbucks is a champion of stellar business practices that strives for social, environmental, and economic benefits for the communities where it does business. The Annual Report further details, "We also believe our Starbucks Global Social Impact strategy, commitments related to ethically sourcing high-quality coffee, contributing positively to the communities we do business in, and being an employer of choice are contributors to our objective." The company makes it clear it is not just about profit, but about elevating partners, customers, suppliers, and the community to create positive action.

Did You Know?

Picking up your morning coffee, you may have heard it or even used the phrase yourself: "I am going to pick up a cup of joe." According to legend, the term *cup of joe* is attributed to former U.S. Navy Secretary Josephus Daniels. After Daniels banned alcohol from Navy vessels in 1914, the soldiers grudgingly began to drink coffee, referring to it as a cup of Joe, or joe.

Great Workplace Environment

It should be no surprise that many people want to work at Starbucks. Starbucks ranked #6 on *Fortune's* 2020 World's Most Admired Companies and was ranked #94 among *Forbes Magazine's* America's Best Large Employers list in 2019. Such high rankings are rightfully earned. The employees Starbucks hires are called *partners*, and the company focuses on its partners, providing opportunities to develop skills, advance careers, and achieve goals. Starbucks has approximately 349,000 partners worldwide, with roughly 228,000 people employed within the United States.

Part-time employees constitute two-thirds of the workforce for Starbucks. They are essential to the company's success and thus are treated with respect. Starbucks offers a multitude of benefits to its eligible full-time and part-time partners, including health care benefits, discounted stock purchase plans, and a matching program, cleverly referred to as Future Roast. Starbucks total pay package is referred to as Your Special Blend because each partner has a unique situation and can make choices within his pay package based on needs and interest. An added plus—all partners get a pound of coffee a week.

Starbucks Careers section on its website reflects the company's strong desire to connect partners and thus customers and the community. The section notes, "We call our employees partners because we are all partners in shared success." Imagine what a powerful impact investing in partners through an inviting culture, superior benefits, and personal development has on customer service. Each partner participates in training, which instills strong coffee education, product expertise, and excellent customer service.

Baristas are the core of the coffee business. The baristas take the lead as they wait on people and work to provide an exceptional customer experience. They custom-mix drinks and explain the origins of different coffees. Starbucks' success is dependent on patrons having a very positive experience in its stores. Partners must not only have the skill and personality to communicate well with customers, but also be knowledgeable about the company's products.

Training is an indelible part of the culture at the coffeehouse. All baristas go through an initial training program, focusing on the skills and knowledge required to be a Starbucks barista. This job training experience enhances customer service and confidence and has a highly successful track record on delivery enhancement. While baristas wear the green apron, there is another level—the black apron—which means the individual is a Coffee Master. A Coffee Master is an expert who can answer detailed questions from customers on the history of coffee, roasting, and origin and prepare a picture-perfect drink, having passed five levels of advanced training.

Did You Know?

In fiscal 2018, the total annual compensation for the Starbucks median employee, a part-time barista in California, was $12,754, including salary and Bean Stock.

Source: Starbucks 2019 Proxy Statement.

Employee Benefits

Starbucks has a history of investing in its partners. While baristas are front and center, the coffeehouse has a multitude of positions available such as store manager, district manager, baker, accounting specialist, sourcing manager, quality assurance manager, senior engineer, and maintenance manager, to name just a few. The pay and perks at the coffee company are good. As a matter of fact, due to the tax overhaul in 2018, Starbucks decided to share $250 million of tax savings with U.S. partners on employee benefits, including a pay raise. Following is a listing of some of the benefits available to eligible part-time and full-time partners:

- Comprehensive Health Coverage. Health insurance covers medical, dental, and vision. Life and disability insurance are also provided to partners.
- Savings. Future Roast, the company's 401(k) retirement plan, includes a generous company match.
- Stock. Partners are offered discounted company stock though Stock Investment Plan (SIP). Participation in the equity reward program, Bean Stock, is available for partners who work in stores and serve customers directly.
- Parental Leave. The generous parental leave policy includes birth and non-birth parents. Adoption-related expenses may be reimbursed up to $10,000 per child for eligible partners.
- Education. The Starbucks College Achievement Plan provides eligible partners in the United States free tuition to earn a bachelor's degree online from Arizona State University.

Intrigued? Check out the total benefits package, available on the Starbucks Career website section, Total Rewards: Your Special Blend. Although the list applies to the United States, Starbucks strives to provide similar benefits to its partners in all countries where it has stores, along with customizing benefits for different regions.

Gender and Racial Pay Equity

Starbucks is committed to its partners, and this includes a commitment of 100 percent pay equity, regardless of gender or race. In March 2018, Starbucks announced it had achieved pay equity for U.S. partners for men and women of all races, and in February 2019, the company announced achieving gender pay equity in China and Canada, two of the company's largest international markets. Starbucks is striving to achieve pay equity on a global scale for all employees.

Starbucks has long been a supporter of equal pay for similar work and, in the last ten years, has made substantial efforts to ensure women and men of all races and ethnicities are compensated in a fair manner. The company has created Equity Principles and Best Practices. These are tools for action, such as:

- Equal footing (do not ask candidates about salary history)
- Transparency (publish pay equity progress annually)
- Accountability (set goals to achieve and maintain 100 percent gender pay equity globally, plus maintaining the 100 percent pay equity in the United States)

Inclusion and Diversity

The culture of Starbucks embraces diversity and recognizes it enhances the work environment. Individuals learn from others with different backgrounds and experience, leading to a stronger, more innovative organization with greater productive capacity. The company website notes:

> At the heart of our business, we seek to inspire and nurture the human spirit—understanding that each person brings a distinct life experience to the table. Our partners are diverse not only in gender, race, ethnicity, sexual orientation, disability, religion and age, but also in cultural backgrounds, life experiences, thoughts and ideas.

Starbucks' long-term commitment to inclusion and diversity has been recognized with a number of esteemed awards. In 2015, 2016, 2017, and 2019, the company was recognized as a Best Place to Work for Disability Inclusion by scoring a perfect 100 score on the Disability Equality Index. Starbucks additionally received a top rating of 100 percent on The Human Rights Campaign 2020 Corporate Equality Index, being a Best Place to Work for LGBTQ Equality, for the tenth year. The company has shown it is a place where everyone is welcome.

One example of its diversity and inclusion efforts is with its hiring goals for military, youth, and refugees. Starbucks is committed to hiring veterans and family members, along with opening military stores at major bases and staffing the stores largely with veterans and military spouses. Opportunity Youth are young people 16–24 years of age who aren't working or in school, and Starbucks recognizes this group as talent untapped and in need of opportunities. The coffeehouse is dedicated to hiring the youth segment, plus providing career development, leadership support, and mentoring for the future workforce. Starbucks is also committed to assisting refugees, a group of individuals who have faced very difficult challenges, with job opportunities and the chance to utilize their talents and rebuild their lives.

Did You Know?

- Starbucks aims to have 25,000 partners graduate from Arizona State University's online program by 2025. (At the end of fiscal 2020, over 4,800 partners graduated.)
- Starbucks expects to hire 25,000 veterans and military spouses by 2025.
- Starbucks anticipates employing 10,000 refugees globally by 2022.
- Starbucks strives to employ 100,000 Opportunity Youth (young people who are not working or in school) by 2020.

Source: Starbucks Proxy Statements.

Contributing to Communities

Starbucks has developed a reputation over the years as a team player. The company is dedicated to making positive contributions to the communities where it does business—it's part of the Starbucks culture. You will regularly find Starbucks partners being good neighbors and giving back to their communities and neighborhoods. Starbucks offers a sizeable workforce to help make the world a better place to live. In fact, in 2017, 125,000 Starbucks partners participated in more than 16,500 projects, which were led by partners and focused on sustainability, hunger, youth, veterans, and refugees. And there has been no slowdown since then, as Starbucks has set a powerful goal of contributing more than 100 percent participation in community service by stores globally by the end of 2020. Over the years, the company has addressed a multitude of causes, but it focuses on strengthening areas where they do business. Partners are active and responsible neighbors in the areas where they live, work, and play. Starbucks believes that "doing good makes good business sense" and the company stores open their doors for community and philanthropic events.

CEO Schultz donated the proceeds of his 1997 book, *Pour Your Heart into It*, in order to start the Starbucks Foundation. At the start, the foundation focused on funding literacy programs and nontraditional education programs. It has since grown by leaps and bounds. According to the company website, "The Starbucks Foundation strengthens communities around the world by advancing opportunities for youth, veterans, refugees and coffee, tea and cocoa farmers and their families, supporting communities affected by disaster, and promoting civic engagement." Today, the Starbucks Foundation is worth $63.3 million and is involved in supporting communities around the globe. The foundation is largely funded by Starbucks and private donations.

Ongoing Starbucks Foundation programs include projects that benefit coffee-, tea-, and cocoa-growing communities; the Ethos Water Fund that supports access to clean water, sanitation, and hygiene education; Partner Matching Grants and Community Service Grants; and Opportunity for Youth, which helps young people aged 16–24 years with career opportunities and life skills. One recipient of the Opportunity for Youth grant gifted from Starbucks is Public Allies Indianapolis. (See sidebar for a discussion on the impact of the Starbucks donation.)

Starbucks Steps Up

The Starbucks Foundation has stepped up to help the global community in response to COVID-19. To date, $9 million has been donated to a variety of initiatives that assist with emergency aid around the world. These include more than $1 million in Neighborhood Grants to more than 400 local organizations in the United States and Canada, $1 million to Feeding America's COVID-19 Response Fund, $1 million to the United Nations Foundation's COVID-19 Solidarity Response Fund, $1 million to the China Soon Ching Ling Foundation, and $1 million to Mercy Corps, which aids coffee and tea communities in Indonesia, Colombia, Guatemala, India, and Ethiopia.

Coffee Talk: *An Interview with Vicki Rubio and Anne-Marie Taylor on the Impact of a Recent Starbucks Donation*

Starbucks Opportunity for Youth Grants have had long-lasting impacts on recipients, organizations, and communities. Vicki Rubio, Public Allies Program Director, and Anne-Marie Taylor, Executive Director of the Indianapolis Neighborhood Resource Center, discuss the impact of Starbucks' recent grant.

What is the organizational purpose of the Indianapolis Neighborhood Resource Center?

The Indianapolis Neighborhood Resource Center (INRC) offers training and technical assistance to help grassroots neighborhood organizations address issues that impact the quality of life in their neighborhoods. INRC strengthens the capacity of neighborhood-based organizations and neighbors to mobilize existing assets, support grassroots leadership, and foster collaboration.

Through training sessions, the provision of technical assistance and individual coaching, INRC supports neighborhood-based organizations as they identify their community's assets and mobilize its capacities. Through this work, grassroots community leaders are creating and strengthening institutions, relationships and processes that support healthy, viable and sustainable communities.

INRC employs three integrated strategies that focus upon developing community assets, encouraging and empowering diverse local, grassroots leadership, promoting collaboration and strengthening neighborhood-based organizations:

Indianapolis Community Building Institute (ICBI). This leadership development program, designed for grassroots community leaders, is a series of workshops focusing on the skills needed to build and grow dynamic neighborhoods. INRC also offers topical and site-based training sessions, bringing resources to neighborhoods to help residents develop the skills they need to lead and create positive change.

Technical Assistance. To meet the specific priorities of neighborhood groups, INRC provides organizational assessments and offers customized technical assistance including neighborhood visioning, referrals, project consultation, asset mapping, courageous conversations, coaching and meeting facilitation.

AmeriCorps Public Allies Indianapolis. INRC serves as the Local Operating Partner for AmeriCorps Public Allies Indianapolis. Public Allies is an AmeriCorps service program that strengthens communities and nonprofits by providing leadership development to local, diverse young leaders who are placed with Indianapolis not-for-profits, helping build organizational capacity.

Vision: INRC envisions a city of connected neighborhoods where residents know their neighbors and relationships are open and constructive. Neighborhoods are locally sustainable, diverse in nature, and have a rich quality of life due to the collective gifts, talents, and dreams of the residents. Neighbors know how to access resources to create their own visions of a healthy neighborhood and are invested in that vision. This investment in neighborhoods allows the City of Indianapolis to become increasingly vibrant and attractive.

How did the INRC begin? Can you share a brief history of the organization?

In 1991, the United Way of Central Indiana (UWCI) and Lilly Endowment, Inc. convened a group to discuss the idea of a training center to build leadership capacity in neighborhoods. In 1993, UWCI requested proposals on behalf of the Coalition for Human Services Planning to create a resource to help support neighborhood organizations. A group of partners that included Community Organizations Legal Assistance Project (COLAP), the Indianapolis Neighborhood Housing Partnership (INHP), Local Initiatives Support Corporation (LISC), and the Marion County Alliance of Neighborhood Associations (MCANA) submitted the selected proposal.

In November 1993, INRC held its first official meeting of the Board of Directors. In January 1994, Indianapolis Mayor Steve Goldsmith issued a press release announcing the formation of INRC to provide training and technical assistance to neighborhood-based organizations. INRC established its headquarters at 1802 N. Illinois Street—a space owned by IU Health. In the 20+ years (January 1994-September 2014) that INRC occupied this space, IU Health provided support in innumerable ways, including: pro bono and discounted remodeling work; dramatically discounted rent (sometimes waiving rent); technical support; and guidance. INRC moved to a new space in 2014 from which it currently operates.

In 1999, INRC was designated as a United Way of Central Indiana agency, as UWCI's strategic plan identified community building as a priority.

In 2008, after a year of internal and external conversations and planning, INRC's Board of Directors voted unanimously to partner with Public Allies, and serve as the Indianapolis Operating Partner, officially launching the planning of Public Allies Indianapolis. On October 16, 2009, a celebration was held to honor the first cohort of 26 men & women who began their Public Allies Indianapolis service. Public Allies Indianapolis will begin our 11th program year in September 2019.

Starbucks donated to the INRC as part of its Opportunity for Youth Grant in 2017–2018 for Public Allies Indianapolis. Can you share a bit about the program and how the Starbucks funding was used?

Public Allies Indianapolis seeks to build a just and equitable society and the diverse leadership to sustain it. We do this by recruiting young people who come from diverse backgrounds educationally, socially, racially, and economically to participate in a 10-month professional development program. The majority of our Allies are between the ages of 18–24 which is within the age group that Starbucks sought to support.

There are three main program components: the nonprofit or public sector apprenticeship, leadership development training, and the Team Service Projects (TSP). Allies serve at an organization providing capacity building support. They participate in weekly trainings that focus on professional development, nonprofit management, and social justice issues. Through the TSP, Allies work with grassroots leaders to create and implement community service projects that reflect the assets and input of the neighborhood. To support Allies in our program, we provide benefits, connections to resources, coaching and supervision. We also provide support to Allies as they transition from the program to higher education, employment, or another year of service. This support includes FAFSA assistance, higher education workshops, mentorship, resume review, mock interviews and connections to employers.

Starbucks funding was used for Ally training and retreats, Ally support roles, community service projects and the Team Service Projects. One particular set of trainings we sought to improve were our race conversations. In the past, we've used different volunteer facilitators to deliver these trainings. Starbucks funding allowed us to hire the Peace Learning Center to create and deliver a curriculum tailored to our group's need. Given the importance and complexity of this topic, it was very valuable for us to have their experienced staff facilitate.

Funding supported Public Allies Indianapolis staff salaries and a contract Master of Social Work advisor for our social work intern, who provided one-on-one coaching to our Allies. With the support of our Resource Coordinator and intern, we were able to connect each Ally who identified barriers to support services including counseling, a financial coach, and housing resources. These connections helped us to retain participants and supported their program success.

We also used funds to host a Community Book Club and Professional Development Day in conjunction with Starbucks.

How has Public Allies impacted Indianapolis? Was the donation impactful?

The Public Allies Indianapolis program impacts Indianapolis through the direct work and support Allies provide to their partner organizations and the community and through the development of each Ally who graduates the program and takes the lessons they learned and uses them to engage in the community and make positive change.

For example, two Allies collaborated to bring domestic violence trainings offered by one organization to a group of women served by the other organization. It was a powerful discussion that allowed the women to share personal stories and learn from and support each other.

A group of Allies, working on their Team Service Project, went out and spoke with residents of the Mars Hill neighborhood to understand what they wanted to see in their community. Residents knew that there were many people in need of food assistance, and there was a local church that operated a community garden. The neighbors wanted to expand the garden to help meet the growing need. They had some active volunteers but needed a capacity boost. The team of Allies worked with the neighbors to determine how to expand the garden and what needed to be done to prep it for the season. The Allies then organized a service day to build additional beds and prepare the current garden for planting. Allies also worked to create a community cookbook filled with recipes that neighbors could use. They helped to build the garden but also to facilitate connection, which is so important for areas to thrive.

As Allies do this work, they are also developing as leaders. They learn about themselves and develop the skills to make change. One Ally spoke of having more patience, spending more time listening to understand rather than respond, and making time to care for herself. Today she works for the same nonprofit where she served as an Ally and is an advocate for safe, affordable housing.

Starbucks support has had a positive impact on our program. Funding from Starbucks allowed us to try new things, like bringing on a social work intern to provide direct support to Allies as they develop in the program and work to pursue their goals. Our community book club was started because of Starbucks and we've appreciated their willingness to engage in conversations on criminal justice reform, racial inequities and the housing and homelessness crisis. Our Starbucks partner has connected us to potential collaborators and has pushed us to think about how we can do more. We value that Starbucks is genuine in wanting to get their employees engaged in the work of the nonprofits they support. We have had great volunteers from Starbucks. The impact of our program has been boosted because of our partnership with Starbucks.

Did You Know?

You probably remember from your history text that in the late 1970s, China began a series of economic reforms, transitioning from a country with a centrally planned government to a market-oriented economy. The reforms have spurred international trade and a growing private sector. During this economic transformation, China packed on some powerful economic statistics.

Here is a quick look at the country. Gross domestic product (GDP) measures the output of a nation's economy—the total market value of all final goods and services produced within a country during a given time frame. Despite a slowdown due to COVID-19, China's economy has experienced stellar growth since the reforms began and, for 2021, projects a robust GDP growth rate of 8.1 percent, contrasted to a respectable 5.1 percent for the United States, according to the International Monetary Funds' *World Economic Outlook*. While the United States has the world's largest economy—at $20 trillion nominal GDP—China is in the number two spot at $14 trillion USD. Furthermore, China is the world's most populous nation with over 1.4 billion people and has a jobless rate of just over 5 percent. One of the world's fastest-growing economies, it is anticipated to be the world's largest economy by 2030, according to Starbucks.

Starbucks opened its first store in China in 1999 and never looked back. Today, China is the company's fastest-growing market. There are now more than 4,700 stores in China with plans of having 6,000 stores by the end of fiscal year 2022. Much of the successful growth can be attributed to the Chief Executive Officer of Starbucks China, Belinda Wong, named #38 in *Fortune's* list of Most Powerful Women in Business International.

Wong introduced a groundbreaking health care plan for the parents of its partners to alleviate the financial stress of health care emergencies. Starbucks tailors benefits to meet the specific needs of partners in different countries, and in China, family is highly important. Traditional values find many children caring for their aging parents. The Starbucks China Parent Care Program, introduced in 2017, covers thirty critical illnesses and some surgeries for parents of eligible partners. This insurance already covers 16,000 parents of Starbucks partners in China and can alleviate the financial stress which often occurs during a family health care emergency.

Supporting Sustainable Commitments

As a leader in the industry, in 2016 Starbucks became a founding member of the Sustainable Coffee Challenge, "helping farmers overcome the challenges facing coffee communities, purchasing ethically sourced coffee, and ensuring the long-term supply of high-quality coffee." Starbucks is doing its part to make sure coffee is sustainable, both assisting the people who produce the coffee and supporting the land on which it grows. The company has stepped up and set a goal of making coffee the first 100 percent sustainable agricultural product. Starbucks is committed to sustainable solutions such as greener power, greener stores, and greener cups to reduce its environmental footprint.

In a Starbucks Story entitled *From Ethical Sourcing to Stores Powered by the Sun* (April 15, 2019), the company outlines four sustainability commitments going from "farms to straws." Following are selected action items:

Responsible Coffee

- Partnering with Conservation International, a nonprofit environmental organization, in committing to purchase 99 percent ethically sourced coffee
- Donating 100 million trees to coffee farmers

Greener Power

- Investing more than $75 million in renewable energy
- Planning to locally source over 50 percent of renewable energy in the United States by 2020

Greener Stores

- Planning to have 10,000 greener stores by 2025
- Opening more than 1,600 LEED-certified stores in twenty countries

Greener Cups and Packaging

- Planning to eliminate plastic straws globally by 2020 and replace with a strawless lid

  Utilizing 10 percent postconsumer fiber in hot cups

To create a more sustainable world, in January 2020, Starbucks announced it will be a planet-positive company. A major commitment, this means that the company has an ambition to give more than it takes from the planet. The company plans to store more carbon than it emits, replenish more clean water than it uses, and eliminate waste. A target goal has been set by the company to reduce carbon, water, and waste footprints in half by 2030.

CHAPTER SEVEN

Financial Results and Executive Leadership

Starbucks is a phenomenon. A very successful and surprising one.
—John Simmons, My Sister's a Barista: How They Made
Starbucks a Home Away from Home (2005)

Coffee Quiz

Guess which famous person ranks #209 on the 2020 Forbes 400 Net Worth list?

A. Elon Musk
B. Travis Kalanick
C. Howard Schultz
D. Jeff Bezos

If you chose C, you are correct. According to *Forbes 400,* an annual ranking of the 400 richest Americans, Starbucks Chairman Emeritus registers at an impressive #209, with a staggering net worth of roughly $3.8 billion. If you are curious, tech entrepreneur Elon Musk is #7 with $68 billion; Uber cofounder Travis Kalanick is #327 with $2.6 billion; and Amazon founder Jeff Bezos is #1 with $179 billion.

What Is a Recession?

Howard Schultz made mention of a "challenging economic environment" when reporting the fiscal 2008 earnings for Starbucks (News

Release: "Starbucks Reports Fourth Quarter and Fiscal 2008 Results," November 10, 2008). Reading between the lines, he was talking about the recession the U.S. economy was experiencing. Shortly thereafter it became official—the United States was in a severe eighteen-month, entrenched recession that began in December 2007 and ran through June 2009. The period was a deep recession coupled with a financial collapse, often referred to as the Great Recession. Let's take a moment to examine what a recession is and who gets to decide if the economy has slowed down so much that a formal determination is made.

The agency that determines if the United States is in a recession is the National Bureau of Economic Research (NBER), a leading nonprofit economic research organization based in Cambridge, Massachusetts. A small group of highly esteemed economists, such as Chairman Robert Hall of Stanford University, Robert Gordon of Northwestern University, and James Poterba, MIT and NBER President, sit on the Business Cycle Dating Committee of the NBER, which makes recession and expansion calls. It is such an important body of economists that even the U.S. government adopts its calls. The function of the Business Cycle Dating Committee is to decide when the nation's economy has reached a peak (high point) or a trough (low point).

A *recession* is a prolonged period of time when a nation's economy is slowing down, or contracting. The Business Cycle Dating Committee explains the multitude of factors that influence a recession:

> Because a recession is a broad contraction of the economy, not confined to one sector, the committee emphasizes economy-wide measures of economic activity. The committee believes that domestic production and employment are the primary conceptual measures of economic activity.
> (Business Cycle Dating Committee, 2008)

During a recession, factory production slows and unemployment rises. Personal income falls as people lose their jobs or work fewer hours. Personal consumption decreases as consumers buy less of everything, particularly luxury items. So a higher-priced gourmet coffee beverage for $4 may be forgone in lieu of an inexpensive, $1 fast-food coffee. The stock market typically falters during depressed economic times too, including Starbucks stock, which dipped downward during the recession.

The good news is that recessions tend to be relatively short-lived. The average recession is just over eleven months long, and the typical expansion period, when economic activity booms, is slightly over fifty-eight months long. When the Business Cycle Dating Committee met via conference call on November 28, 2008, the committee determined that a peak in economic activity had occurred in the U.S. economy in December 2007. The peak marks the end of the expansion that began in November 2001 and the beginning of a recession. On September 20, 2010, the Business Cycle Dating Committee announced, after studying profuse economic data, that a trough in economic activity occurred in June 2009. The trough marks the end of the recession and the beginning of an expansion, which we are currently experiencing. A recession begins when the economy reaches a peak of activity and ends when the economy reaches its trough. Between trough and peak, the economy is in an expansion.

During this eighteen-month recession, the longest of any recession since World War II, a host of economic indicators tumbled. The major macroeconomic indicators were hit hard. Gross domestic product, which measures the total output of the economy, typically trends near the 3 percent growth rate. During the recession, output was stagnant and often declining, hitting a negative 7.2 percent in the last quarter of 2008. The unemployment rate, which was 5 percent at the beginning of the recession, rose to 9.5 percent for June 2009, topping out at a full 10 percent in October 2009. Inflation, a sustained increase in prices, which usually declines during a downturn, still had some modest uptick. You get the idea—a very bad combination of economic occurrences.

The financial effects hit consumers in a number of ways, particularly in the area of home ownership. Homeowners saw a substantial reduction in the value of their homes, and homes became much harder to sell, some sitting on the market without a sale for years. The recession resulted in a depressed economic environment in virtually every business sector. But what was the origin of this recession? The cause of the economic downturn in the United States was multifold, but one key factor was the subprime problem. Plain and simple, some financial institutions made mortgage loans to customers who simply did not have the job security and financial wherewithal to repay the loans. According to a Chicago Fed Letter, between 2007 and 2010, there were roughly 3.8 million home foreclosures.

Exacerbating the problem, these subprime mortgages were bundled up together into bonds and sold to major institutional investors around the globe—including insurance companies, pension funds, and huge financial institutions. These faltering investments with their resulting losses crippled the financial markets both domestically and globally. The credit market was tight, and commercial bank lending came to a screeching halt. With business activity down and many individuals without a job, people were cutting their budgets and, yes, rethinking high-end coffee purchases.

You Decide—Sell the Jet?

You'll find no argument about whether Starbucks was hit by the downturn in the economy. But while earnings significantly faltered, the company still remained profitable. The management team took a head-on approach to keeping the company strong and viable. One of the tactics the company seriously engaged to remain a viable business is cutting costs. That meant closing stores, cutting jobs, and yes, putting all three of the corporate jets up for sale. In December 2008, Starbucks took delivery of its new Gulfstream 550—a $45 million jet. The company had placed the order three years earlier and would have been hit with huge fees for canceling the order. The Gulfstream 550 is a long-range aircraft and can accommodate up to nineteen passengers. Three years prior, when the order was placed, the economy was in an expansion period and the company stock price was bolstered. The Starbucks jet was lightly used, to say the least, having made only fifteen flights.

Even before the new plane was delivered, Starbucks had already placed its seven-year-old Gulfstream V up for sale. And according to a March 6, 2009, article in the *Seattle Times*, the company also wanted to sell its third plane, a five-year-old Challenger 604 by Bombardier that accommodates ten.

Why have corporate jets? One side of the debate says executives are busy and it makes more sense economically to use a corporate jet. Their time is worth money. The private jet is, in a sense, an office where execs can work and exchange ideas. Commercial flights can be time wasting and often result in delays and cancellations. With a private jet, an executive can have a meeting on the opposite coast in the morning and be assured he'll be back the same day for a late-afternoon board meeting at headquarters. For Starbucks, which at the time had over 16,000 stores in 46 countries outside the United States, the efficiency argument was strong.

The other side of the coin says corporate jets are an excess—an extravagance useful only for the corporate ego. The millions of dollars devoted to the lavish travel style they represent are not a good use of corporate funds in good economic times or troubled. Executives can drive or take commercial flights when needed or corporate jets can be leased.

The down economy played hardball with the aviation market during the recession. Put on top of that the recent venting against corporate air travel, and you have huge aircraft inventories and jet prices that dropped by 30 percent or more because of the flood of used jets on the market. When CEOs from the Detroit 3 automakers flew to the nation's capital in private planes to testify before Congress in 2009, it caused quite an uproar. The ironic reason? While still enjoying luxurious private travel, the troubled automakers were there to discuss multibillion-dollar government loan assistance. While Ford did not seek short-term financial assistance from the government, GM and Chrysler did receive emergency funding. Likely in order to calm the extreme public relations debacle, GM and Ford announced they would sell their fleets of corporate jets. Chrysler was leasing its jets from an aircraft operator.

What do you think? If you were the executive of a big company, would you make the same decision and place your fleet of planes up for sale? Do you think the executive staff will lose much efficiency by driving and having to take commercial airlines? If you were traveling across the United States and overseas on business, would you charter a private jet? Think about your plans and strategies for company travel.

Strategic Moves to Rebound

After stepping down from day-to-day activities in 2000 to become chairman, it was in January 2008 that Howard Schultz returned to Starbucks as its CEO, replacing Jim Donald. Schultz knew that the company had expanded store growth rapidly and had lost its connection to the customer. Add that to the devastating economic picture emerging in the United States, and some customers were gravitating to cheaper coffee options. Schultz noted, "We thought in terms of millions of customers and thousands of stores instead of one customer, one partner, and one cup of coffee at a time" (Onward, p. 97). Schultz was once again at the head of the company to lead in a two-year major restructuring initiative and recessionary repositioning. The global retailer had experienced declining U.S. store traffic, rising milk prices, a depressed stock price, and faltering sales. Starbucks' job was to learn to operate efficiently during an economic downturn.

The company was up to the challenge, addressing the difficult economic times head-on. Starbucks launched an extreme transitional strategy. By cutting costs and focusing on customer-based initiatives, the coffee company cut $580 million in costs for fiscal 2009. How did it accomplish such a daunting task?

Following are a few of the more notable cost-cutting items:

- Hundreds of underperforming stores closed.
- New store expansion slowed.
- Some funds allocated for U.S. stores were moved into international expansion.
- Thousands of jobs were cut.
- Some stores stopped brewing decaf after noon to better control waste.
- The $45 million company jet was put up for sale.
- Schultz requested a cut in his base salary from $1.2 million to $10,000.

Following are some transformational ideas employed:

- MyStarbucksidea.com launched.
- Training for partners was beefed up.
- A new selection of economical coffee-and-breakfast pairings was introduced.
- New products, including the milder Pike Place Roast coffee, were introduced.
- Rewards were added to the Starbucks card.
- Hot sandwiches were eliminated which concealed coffee aroma.
- In-store coffee grinding was revived.

Lessons Learned

A roller coaster ride, comparable store sales growth moved from 7 percent in 2006, 5 percent in 2007, dipping to –3 percent in 2008, –6 percent in 2009, and rebounding to 7 percent in 2010. The two-year transformational journey that began in 2008 when Howard Schultz returned as CEO saw the 2010 revenues increase to a record $10.7 billion. Comparable store sales, or same-store sales, a vital measurement for financial analysts and investors, comparing one year's sales in retail stores to the same period the previous year, was back to the pre-recession level of 7 percent. Starbucks learned to watch costs, critique expansion plans carefully, and make a bigger effort to be tuned in to customer needs. The company became a leaner, more efficiently run business. These were good lessons to learn because the company must be prepared for the cyclical nature of the economy and be ready for the next recession.

Howard Schultz summarized the situation as he began the Starbucks biennial investor meeting on December 4, 2008, a date when virtually all businesses were feeling depressed sales:

> Things are going to get better. People will continue to drink coffee, and the equity of our brand and the relevancy of the sense of community in the third place and the growth opportunities for Starbucks, domestically and around the world, will be stronger than ever.
>
> (*Onward*, p. 230)

Through quick action, cost-cutting activities, and reconnecting with the customers, Schultz was correct, and things did get better. And yes, people continue to drink coffee, craving the Starbucks high-quality brew.

Starbucks Experiments with $1 Coffee

On January 23, 2008, *The Wall Street Journal* reported that Starbucks was testing a $1 cup of coffee, as well as free refills on some brews, as part of a trial run in Seattle. That was about 50 cents less than what the short brew would regularly sell for at that time, although prices vary from store to store. An eight-ounce short brew at the test price rivals even McDonald's and Dunkin', companies that have heaped some heavy competition on the global coffee giant as of late. At the time, both of these fierce fast-food competitors started their coffee prices in the low- to mid-$1 range.

The initiative apparently created some buzz. In a Starbucks transformation agenda press release (January 30, 2008), Schultz commented:

> We have received a lot of attention in the last week about the $1 brewed coffee 8-ounce short test. Testing is a way of life for us as we continue to find ways to enhance the customer experience. Right now, as a test, it makes sense to us. I'd like to reiterate that Starbucks is built on premium coffee and a premium experience. We intend to maintain our leadership position at the high end, while broadening our appeal. And similar to other leading global consumer brands, we believe there are opportunities to create market segmentation, provide an entry point for new customers, and generate trial in a way that will also maintain the value of our core brand proposition.

In the end, that is all it was—a test lasting just one month. Although the $1 Starbucks coffee did not become standard fare, the short-term experiment was well received and created a great deal of excitement from customers. Testing, challenging assumptions, looking at a new perspective, and breaking the mold can all lead to creative new ways to build a business.

Starbucks Coffee Pricing

The response of a consumer to a change in price is measured by an economic concept called *price elasticity of demand*. It is a numerical measure that helps explain people's behavior and a useful tool for economists doing research or a company making pricing decisions. The price elasticity of demand is measured by dividing the *percentage change in quantity demanded* by the *percentage change in price*. The mathematical measurement looks like this:

Price Elasticity (E) = % change in quantity demanded ÷ % change in price

Demand is elastic when the percentage change in price causes a greater percentage change in quantity demanded. If the absolute value of price elasticity is larger than 1, demand is elastic. Consumers respond significantly to a change in price. Big purchases like dishwashers, cars, and televisions tend to be sensitive to price changes and are elastic.

Demand is inelastic when the percentage change in quantity demanded is less than the percentage change in price. If the absolute value of price elasticity is between 0 and 0.99, demand is inelastic. Necessity items, like coffee, prescription drugs, milk, and gasoline (over the short term), all tend to be relatively insensitive to a price change. This is referred to as inelastic, and consumers are not extremely sensitive to a price increase. Knowing that a good has inelastic demand suggests that a company should consider increasing prices.

If demand is elastic, a price hike will mean lower total revenue. On the other hand, for products with an inelastic demand, it will increase the bottom line to raise prices within a certain level. The customers who frequent Starbucks may be quite insensitive to price changes, a highly inelastic demand, and a small increase in price can have a large impact on the company revenues.

While Starbucks pricing decisions are massive, the concept can be seen with a smaller example. Consider a local coffeehouse where the coffee price has been set at $2 a cup, and daily sales are 200 brews per day. The store is considering a rate increase to $2.50 a cup, and daily sales are projected to fall to 195 cups. At $2 a cup and 200 cups, there is $400 total revenue. But changing the price to $2.50 and multiplied by 195 cups equals a total revenue of $487.50. Daily revenue is projected to go up a total of $87.50. The numerical elasticity measurement also shows an inelastic measurement. The price will change a total of $0.50 ÷ $2.25 = 0.22. To compute the percent change in quantity demanded, it is 5 ÷ 197.50 = 0.03. The measurement is inelastic at 0.03 ÷ 0.22 = 0.14. This tells us that a 1 percent increase in coffee prices triggers just a 0.14 percent fall in purchases. This makes it a wise decision to increase the per-cup price.

Price elasticity can be used to determine whether loyal coffee drinkers are willing to spend more money on their beverage when the price is increased. If a company knows they have an inelastic demand, then they would never want to lower the price because total revenue would fall. Starbucks prices can vary quite a bit at different locations, and periodically they do increase the price of beverages. An article from the June 7, 2018 issue of *Business Insider* noted that Starbucks had just raised the price of brewed coffee by 10–20 cents across sizes at most of the company store locations. A tall brewed coffee rose to $1.95–$2.15, and many of the fancier drinks to near $5 a cup. While coffee is an inelastic good, many believe there are few, if any, substitutes for Starbucks coffee, thus making the demand for the brand itself highly inelastic. Even a small increase in price can cause company revenues to soar.

Starbucks Financial Overview

After a decade plus of robust economic growth the COVID-19 pandemic forced the economy into an abrupt halt, causing the United States to officially enter a recession in February 2020. The downturn was the first since the last recession ended in June 2009. An examination of the company's financials during the 2016–2020 period will highlight the exceptional growth coupled with the downturn impact. It is important to examine the revenue and income numbers over a trend period to get a better perspective on the impressive growth this company has seen overall. The key factor is that the company's fundamentals are sound. Quality arabica coffee—with over thirty blends and single-origin premiums available—is a great product, and people will keep drinking coffee, along with tea and all the other wonderful specialty drinks. Consumers will continue to eat—this we know for sure. Starbucks plans to stay at the forefront of the food-and-beverage industry. The company has all the ingredients for long-term success in place—a quality product, a strong brand name, sound core financials, a top-notch management team, and a highly experienced big-business board of directors.

While typically on an upward climb with revenues, fiscal year 2020 displays the force of COVID-19. In the 10-K 2020 for Starbucks Kevin Johnson, CEO and President, pointed out, "Starbucks results for fiscal 2020 reflect the challenges our business faced with the COVID-19 pandemic, which severely impacted our results, particularly during the second and third fiscal quarters."

As you can see from Table 7.1, Starbucks has indeed set a strong foundation for growth. Assets valued at $14.3 billion for fiscal 2016 have more than doubled for fiscal 2020, at $29.4 billion. Net earnings amounted to $924 million in fiscal 2020, severely curtailed from the $2.8 billion recorded in fiscal 2016. Earnings per share for fiscal 2020 was just $0.79 compared to $2.92 for the previous year. During each of the three quarters of fiscal 2020, the company paid a cash dividend to shareholders of $0.41 per share, a total of $1.23. A good sign of confidence by the board

Table 7.1 Starbucks: Key Financial Data, 2016–2020

	Fiscal 2020	Fiscal 2019	Fiscal 2018	Fiscal 2017	Fiscal 2016
Net Revenue	$23.5 billion	$26.5 billion	$24.7 billion	$22.4 billion	$21.3 billion
Net Earnings including non-controlling interests*	$924 million	$3.6 billion	$4.5 billion	$2.9 billion	$2.8 billion
EPS-diluted*	$0.79	$2.92	$3.24	$1.97	$1.90
Cash dividend per share**	$1.23	$1.49	$1.32	$1.05	$0.85
Total Assets	$29.4 billion	$19.2 billion	$24.2 billion	$14.4 billion	$14.3 billion

* Fiscal 2018 results include a gain not subject to income tax of $1.4 billion resulting from the acquisition of the East China joint venture. The impact of the gain to our diluted EPS was $0.99.
** Subsequent to year-end, on September 30, 2020, company declared a cash dividend of $0.45 per share payable on November 27, 2020 to shareholders of record on November 12, 2020.
Source: Starbucks 10-K 2020.

of directors on September 30, 2020, the board of directors approved an increase from $0.41 per share to $0.45 per share, with the dividend payment to be distributed on November 27, 2020 (after the fiscal year closed). This action will raise the annual dividend to $1.80.

In a positive, uplifting commentary, Johnson spoke about the future for the coffee giant, at the Q4 2020 Earnings Call:

> The guiding principles we established at the onset of the pandemic, combined with our industry-leading digital platform and our ability to innovate rapidly, continue to fuel our recovery and provide confidence in a robust operating outlook for fiscal 2021. Our strategies are working and I am optimistic that we will emerge from the COVID-19 pandemic as a stronger and more resilient company.

At the earnings release of Q4 2020 and the fiscal year 2020, the company provided key points on forward guidance, or hopes for fiscal 2021. Forward guidance is the guidance provided by public companies during quarterly earnings announcements, providing a firm's projections for the upcoming year (or quarter) on earnings, revenue, and select financial numbers. The fiscal year for 2021 is a fifty-three-week year instead of the usual fifty-two weeks. Clearly, the company is planning a strong recovery and has confidence in the outlook for fiscal 2021 and coming years. Following are some of the notable forward guidance points for fiscal 2021.

- Consolidated revenue of $28.0 billion to $29.0 billion, inclusive of a $500 million impact attributable to the fifty-third week
- Generally Accepted Accounting Principles (GAAP) EPS in the range of $2.34 to $2.54 in fiscal 2021, including approximately $0.10 for the fifty-third week
- Non-GAAP EPS in the range of $2.70 to $2.90 for full year, inclusive of a $0.10 impact attributable to the fifty-third week
- A net 1,100 new Starbucks stores globally (approximately 600 of these net new stores in China)

The Stores

Starbucks is a big-time coffee retailer; at the end of fiscal 2020, it had 32,660 stores. As a comparison, a decade earlier in fiscal 2010, the company touted 16,858 stores. In ten years, Starbucks nearly doubled its store count. The company-owned and licensed stores (typically with well-known retailers) generate most of Starbucks' revenue, while additional sources such as sales of packaged coffee, tea, and ready-to-drink beverages outside of the stores have an impact, as well. The only word that can be used to describe Starbucks' growth is *astronomical*, considering the humble beginnings in 1971, when the company was founded with one store in Seattle.

It was in 1996 that Starbucks forayed into the international arena, opening its first international store in Japan. And while Japan had 1,464 company-operated stores at the end of fiscal 2020, China's number stood at 4,704, a market the company just entered in 1999. Today, it is China that takes center stage and is currently the fastest-growing market overall for the company. Opportunities abound in China, and Starbucks is ready to play. China, traditionally a country of tea drinkers, is seeing coffee consumption on the rise. Last year alone, according to the USDA's Foreign Agricultural Service, coffee imports to China grew 16 percent, compared to total country import growth of roughly 3.8 percent. An epic surge, Starbucks is opening 600 stores a year in China. This approximates to one store every 15 hours. And when the company celebrated a major milestone on May 18, 2019, the opening of its 30,000th store, where do you think it was located? You guessed it—China. Shenzhen, China to be specific.

Growing the store base remains essential to the brand, and uplifting existing stores in new and inspiring ways accelerates Starbucks' growth. While Starbucks strives to keep net new store growth around 6–7 percent each year, some stores must be closed in the process. When it was announced that Starbucks planned to close company-operated stores, the closures typically are due to underperforming establishments. The goal for fiscal 2021 is a whopping 1,150 net new stores globally. Growth in new stores, along with some necessary closures, was all done in pursuit of company health. Table 7.2 displays the exceptional growth for company-operated stores in China during just one fiscal year. A very challenging year, fiscal 2020 had net new stores of 581. The growth for fiscal 2021 is projected to be 600 net stores in China, with openings and closings.

Looking back on Starbucks' tough 2020, as well as their constant streamlining and finetuning of both products, digital methodologies, and stores, shows the company strategy has been successful. They still top the competition for coffee sales. Continued strategic investment is part of their long-term plan for profitable growth and future opportunities.

Table 7.2   **Starbucks Company-Operated Store Data China**

Stores open as of September 29, 2019	4,123
Opened during the fiscal year	613
Closed during the fiscal year	(32)
Net stores	581
Stores open as of September 27, 2020	4,704

Source: Starbucks 10-K 2020.

Starbucks has a goal of 6,000 stores in China by the end of 2022, one they will likely surpass.

Executive Team

Executive officers are the top leaders of a corporation. This group is in charge of running the company on a daily basis. The chief executive officer (CEO) is the top position—the person in charge of the overall management of a company. Additionally, the CEO is responsible for reporting to the board of directors.

One huge advantage that Starbucks has is its skilled executive leadership. This top-notch team of execs is led by a man with a vision, Kevin Johnson, who is the president and CEO of the company, and a director since 2009. Howard Schultz, the founder of the new Starbucks, stepped down as CEO in April 2017, when Johnson succeeded him as president and CEO. In 1987, Schultz, along with a group of investors, purchased Starbucks Coffee Company's six stores and he never looked back. Schultz, a charismatic leader with a spectacular vision for new beverage and food products, was chairman of the board and CEO from 1986 to 2000 and again from 2008 to 2017, along with being executive chairman from 2017 to 2018.

On June 26, 2018, Howard Schultz retired from the company and was granted the honorary title of Chairman Emeritus by the board. Schultz was a strong leader, iconic director, and visionary and is overwhelmingly credited for the success of Starbucks. Johnson, a leader with similar vision, strength, and forward momentum, set out to position the company for long-term sustainable growth. While Johnson will continue to drive global revenue and global comparable store sales, watch for the company's next wave of growth to be focused in the Chinese market.

Table 7.3 **Starbucks Executive Compensation, 2020**

Name and Principal Position	Salary	Stock/ Option	Other	Total
Kevin R. Johnson, President and CEO	$1,540,379	$11,166,708	$1,958,488	$14,665,575
Patrick J. Grismer, Exec. VP and CFO	$889,149	$2,698,061	$697,420	$4,284,900
Rosalind G. Brewer, Group President Americas & COO	$1,065,200	$4,802,284	$1,340,450	$7,207,934
Lucy Helm, Exec. VP, Chief Partner Officer (retired on October 30, 2020, replaced by Angela Lis)	$654,233	$3,396,425	$371,035	$4,421,693
John Culver, Group President, International, Channel Development and Global Coffee & Tea	$912,113	$4,802,284	$752,058	$6,466,454

Source: Starbucks 2021 Proxy Statement.

In the following paragraphs, you will find biographical descriptions of select Starbucks senior executives as taken from the company's Fiscal 2020 10-K, filed with the U.S. Securities and Exchange Commission. Note that Angela Lis succeeds Lucy Helm, following her retirement in late 2020. As you will see, Johnson has a group of high-powered and experienced executive officers working with him. Johnson is a skilled leader, but he also directs a competent and talented executive team—by all accounts, an experienced team with a proven record at Starbucks and with other major companies worldwide. A talented executive team is essential for the continued health of Starbucks, and this group looks to have the credentials to weather any economic storm.

Kevin R. Johnson, Age 60, President and CEO

Kevin R. Johnson has served as president and chief executive officer since April 2017 and has been a Starbucks director since March 2009. Johnson served as president and chief operating officer from March 2015 to April 2017. He served as chief executive officer of Juniper Networks, Inc., a leading provider of high-performance networking products and services, from September 2008 to December 2013. He also served on the board of directors of Juniper Networks from September 2008 through February 2014. Prior to joining Juniper Networks, he served as President, Platforms and Services Division, for Microsoft Corporation, a worldwide provider of software, services, and solutions. He was a member of Microsoft's Senior Leadership Team and held several senior executive positions over the course of his sixteen years at Microsoft. Prior to joining Microsoft in 1992, he worked in International Business Machine Corp.'s systems integration and consulting business.

Five Fascinating Facts about Kevin Johnson

1. His mother was a pediatric nurse and his father, a theoretical physicist.
2. Graduated from New Mexico State University in 1981, returned in 2017 to receive an Honorary Doctorate.
3. Served on the National Telecommunications Advisory Committee under Presidents George W. Bush and Barack Obama.
4. His great-grandfather's pocket watch is one of his prized possessions.
5. Grew up in a small town, Los Alamos, New Mexico, which has a population of just over 12,000.

Patrick J. Grismer, Age 58, Executive Vice President and CFO

Patrick J. Grismer joined Starbucks in November 2018 as executive vice president, chief financial officer. From March 2016 to November 2018, he served as executive vice president, chief financial officer of Hyatt Hotels Corporation, a global hospitality company. From May 2012 to February 2016, he served as chief financial officer at Yum! Brands, Inc., a global restaurant company. He previously held a number of roles at Yum!, including chief planning and control officer and chief financial officer for Yum! Restaurants International. Prior to that, he served in various roles at the Walt Disney Company including vice president, Business Planning and Development, for the Disneyland Resort and chief financial officer for the Disney Vacation Club. Grismer began his career with Price Waterhouse.

Rosalind G. Brewer, Age 58, Group President Americas and COO

Rosalind G. Brewer has served as group president, Americas and chief operating officer since October 2017 and has been a director of

Starbucks since March 2017. Ms. Brewer served as president and chief executive officer of Sam's Club, a membership-only retail warehouse club and a division of Walmart Inc., a multinational retail corporation, from February 2012 to February 2017. Previously, she was executive vice president and president of Walmart's East Business Unit from February 2011 to January 2012; executive vice president and president of Walmart South from February 2010 to February 2011; senior vice president and division president of the Southeast Operating Division from March 2007 to January 2010; and regional general manager, Georgia Operations, from 2006 to February 2007. Prior to joining Walmart, she was president of Global Nonwovens Division for Kimberly-Clark Corporation, a global health and hygiene products company, from 2004 to 2006, and held various management positions at Kimberly-Clark Corporation from 1984 to 2006. She currently serves as the chair of the board of trustees for Spelman College and as a director on the board of directors of Amazon.com, Inc. She formerly served on the board of directors for Lockheed Martin Corporation and Molson Coors Brewing Company.

Angela Lis, Age 53, Executive Vice President and Chief Partner Officer

Angela Lis joined Starbucks in 1992 as a part-time barista and has served as executive vice president and chief partner officer since November 2, 2020. From September 2016 to October 2020, Ms. Lis served as senior vice president, global business partners. In this role she was responsible for talent and partner strategies that drive our global retail operations business. Prior to this role, she served as a vice president of partner resources for corporate business functions and global supply chain. During her tenure at Starbucks, she has led partner resources business partners across the globe. She has supported both retail and all non-retail business units and was instrumental in the start-up of our Channel Development business.

John Culver, Age 60, Group President, International, Channel Development and Global Coffee & Tea

John Culver joined Starbucks in August 2002 and has served as group president, International, Channel Development and Global Coffee & Tea, since July 2018. From October 2017 to July 2018, Mr. Culver served as group president, International and Channels. From September 2016 to October 2017, he served as group president, Starbucks Global Retail. From May 2013 to September 2016, he served as group president, China,

Asia Pacific, Channel Development and Emerging Brands. He served as president, Starbucks Coffee China and Asia Pacific, from October 2011 to May 2013. From December 2009 to October 2011, he served as president, Starbucks Coffee International. He served as executive vice president; president, Global Consumer Products, Foodservice and Seattle's Best Coffee from February 2009 to September 2009, and then as president, Global Consumer Products and Foodservice, from October 2009 to November 2009. He previously served as senior vice president; president, Starbucks Coffee Asia Pacific, from January 2007 to February 2009, and vice president; general manager, Foodservice, from August 2002 to January 2007. Mr. Culver serves on the board of directors of Kimberly-Clark Corporation.

Board of Directors

A board of directors is made up of individuals, elected by shareholders of a business, who have ultimate governing authority. These individuals make decisions for the company on behalf of the owners. In general, it is the board's job to take care of the big business decisions, such as establishing corporate management policies, appointing senior management, approving executive compensation, determining dividend and options policies, and deciding if a merger or acquisition would be advantageous for the company.

The Starbucks board of directors has adopted governance principles and committee charters to lead the company. The Starbucks Corporate Governance Principles and Practices for the board of directors read as follows:

> The fundamental responsibility of the company's Board of Directors is to promote the best interests of the company and its shareholders by overseeing the management of the company's business affairs. In doing so, board members have two basic legal obligations to the company and its shareholders: (1) the duty of care, which generally requires that board members exercise appropriate diligence in making decisions and in overseeing management of the company; and (2) the duty of loyalty, which generally requires that board members make decisions based on the best interests of the company and its shareholders, without regard to personal interest.

Members of a board usually include senior executives from the company, who are called *inside directors*. Johnson, for example, sits on the board and serves as the company's CEO and president. *Outside directors,* as the other board members are called, are highly respected individuals from the community. At the March 17, 2021, annual meeting the company is slated to elect twelve members to sit on the board. Starbucks Corporate Governance Principles and Practices state, "The board shall meet at least five times during the fiscal year, and may hold more meetings if necessary or appropriate."

Let's take a look at the high-level group of individuals governing this organization: the Starbucks Corporation board of directors. You will see the expansive breadth of big-business leadership these individuals bring to the table. Also notably, many members carry longevity of service on the board, lending insightful expertise to ensure the continued success of the Starbucks mission.

In fiscal 2018, Howard Schultz retired from his executive position with Starbucks and was award the title of Chairman Emeritus. Upon Schultz's retirement, Myron E. (Mike) Ulman, III was named chairman and Mellody Hobson was named vice chair of the board. Ullman, former head of retail giant J.C. Penney, and Hobson, who in July 2019 was appointed as co-CEO of money management firm Ariel Investments, LLC, bring high-level business expertise to the Starbucks board.

For the 2020 plan year, compensation program (March 2020 to March 2021) for nonemployee directors provided total annual compensation for nonemployee directors of $295,000 per year. The previous plan year's total annual compensation for nonemployee directors was a total of $270,000.

The Starbucks board members represent a variety of perspectives and skills from the group's stellar business and professional experience. Notice you won't find anyone over age 75 on the board. There is mandatory retirement immediately before the company's annual meeting during the calendar year when a board member turns 75. This is done in an effort to keep professionals on the board who are in tune with the work environment of today.

The Chair, Myron E. Ullman, III, has reached the mandatory retirement age and will not be eligible for re-election. If re-elected Mellody Hobson will become the next independent chair of the board of directors.

Starbucks Corporation Board of Directors Nominees

Richard E. Allison, Jr., age 53, Director since 2019
Chief Executive Officer and Director of Domino's Pizza, Inc.

Rosalind G. Brewer, age 58, Director since 2017

Group President, Americas and Chief Operating Officer of Starbucks Corporation

Andrew Campion, age 49, Director since 2019

Chief Operating Officer of NIKE, Inc.

Mary N. Dillon, age 59, Director since 2016

Chief Executive Officer and Director of Ulta Beauty, Inc.

Isabel Ge Mahe, age 46, Director since 2019

Vice President and Managing Director of Greater China of Apple, Inc.

Mellody Hobson, age 51, Director since 2005

Co-Chief Executive Officer and President and Director of Ariel Investments, LLC

Kevin R. Johnson, age 60, Director since 2009

President and Chief Executive Officer of Starbucks Corporation

Jørgen Vig Knudstorp, age 52, Director since 2017

Executive Chairman of LEGO Brand Group

Satya Nadella, age 53, Director since 2017

Chief Executive Officer and Director of Microsoft Corporation

Joshua Cooper Ramo, age 52, Director since 2011

Chairman and Chief Executive Officer of Somay

Clara Shih, age 39, Director since 2011

Executive Chairperson and Director of Hearsay Systems, Inc.

Javier G. Teruel, age 70, Director since 2005

Retired Vice Chairman of Colgate-Palmolive Company

Annual Stockholders Meetings

Annual meetings are important events because they represent an annual review of a company's performance and provide insight into future business activities. This keeps stockholders abreast of future plans and allows them to vote on important company actions, such as electing new members to the board of directors. Starbucks' annual meetings are ticketed events open to all shareholders and are highly anticipated extravaganzas. Surprise musical guest and three-time Grammy Award winner Brandi Carlile performed onstage for stockholders at the 2019 meeting. Shareholders experienced raking green coffee beans on a replica patio, and guests consumed 2,608 short cups of coffee.

The 2019 annual meeting of shareholders was held on March 20, 2019, when over 3,900 shareholders gathered at WaMu Theater in downtown Seattle. They went to listen to Starbucks leader Kevin Johnson, and other key executives, review the financials and unveil the company's new initiatives to grow the business while elevating customers and partners. Following are five major highlights noted at the annual meeting, where revenue of nearly $25 billion was announced, the largest in history:

- Starbucks will reimagine the Third Place vision by listening to the customer and focusing on three attributes: convenience, comfort, and connection.
- The company will support its innovative agenda by investing $100 million in Valor Siren Ventures, a private equity group which identifies and funds early stage growth companies for food and retail.
- For the second consecutive year, Starbucks maintained 100 percent gender and race equity pay in the United States, and now China and Canada have joined the United States in committing to pay equity principles.
- Customers will eventually be able to trace the journey of their coffee from the bean to the cup, utilizing the mobile app.
- The company has created a new strawless cold lid which will aid in eliminating plastic straws in stores by 2020.

A detailed press release from the company, with a summary of the annual meeting, was released that same day. The CEO and president assured stockholders, "Starbucks is a different kind of company—and we have been since our founding," Johnson proudly noted. "Our long-term plan for growth with focus and discipline is built on the acknowledgement that the pursuit of profit is not in conflict with the pursuit of doing good. We are a part of millions of people's everyday lives around the world, and I believe we are uniquely positioned to be one of the most enduring brands of all time."

The annual meeting planned for March 18, 2020, was rescheduled from WaMu Theater to a virtual meeting in an effort to maintain safety in the midst of the COVID-19 pandemic. President and CEO Kevin Johnson stressed the focus on health and resiliency: "And today I have a different agenda, an agenda that speaks to all Starbucks stakeholders. This includes my Starbucks partners, the hundreds of millions of Starbucks customers around the world, the thousands of communities we serve and our loyal shareholders." He continued, "We do this knowing this situation is temporary and Starbucks is resilient." At the virtual get-togethers business matters were still addressed, although in an abbreviated format. The meeting concentrated on health and safety concerns, mobilizing digital delivery, and recovery and growth in and outside of the China market. Following are some key numeric highlights about the China market:

1. Over 90 percent of Starbucks stores in China are open, under reduced hours and conditions.
2. Starbucks is committed to growth in China, where it has a goal of 6,000 stores by 2022.
3. The company s announced a $130 million investment in China for a Coffee Innovation Park outside of Shanghai, for a roasting warehouse and distribution facility.

Johnson positively expressed, "Now the next 12 months will be full of adventure in what I call, the road to our 50th, where together we will celebrate the 50th Anniversary of the Starbucks Coffee Company."

Annual stockholder meetings for Starbucks are held in March of each year. The March 17, 2021, meeting is a virtual webcast. Investors, analysts, and interested individuals may read the meeting transcript along with a host of other financial documents at the Starbucks Investor Relations website at https://www.investor.starbucks.com.

CHAPTER EIGHT

Coffee Competition

Now, in this competitive landscape, given the large and growing address-able market around premium coffee, we're seeing more competition enter the market, it's to be expected.

—Kevin Johnson, President and CEO Starbucks,
Starbucks Investor Day (December 13, 2018)

Did You Know?

Over 2 billion cups of coffee are consumed in the world every day.

Source: Unpacking Coffee podcast.

The Mom-and-Pop Cafes

No doubt you have heard it before: Starbucks puts small, mom-and-pop coffeehouses out of business. Critics argue that the global coffeehouse doesn't play fair. They maintain that the coffee company targets small coffeehouses by saturating the market with closely spaced Starbucks stores, buying out competitors' leases, or paying premiums for real estate that small coffeehouses cannot afford. These practices all mark small businesses for failure and force them out. Consumers lose because there is less competition; fewer choices result in higher prices. The company has been dubbed anticompetitive by some. Starbucks does have a strategy to achieve and maintain a dominant market position, but this is a highly debated issue in coffee circles, so let's examine both sides of the debate, and you can be the judge.

The other side of the coin is that some local mom-and-pop stores are actually helped by Starbucks. The company has deep pockets and does a tremendous amount of advertising. The mom-and-pop stores don't always have money in their budgets for ads, but Starbucks has increased knowledge about and awareness of coffee and specialty blends for everybody in the industry. Small coffee shops may see some positive spin-off effects from Starbucks' very presence. According to a recent publication of the National Coffee Association (NCA), specialty coffee drinkers consumed 2.24 cups of coffee a day in 2001, and by 2017 the number rose to 2.97 cups a day. Starbucks just might have increased business for all establishments selling gourmet coffee, big and small alike. Years ago, a cup of coffee was just a way to wake up in the morning or stay alert at night; Starbucks has made drinking coffee into a culture.

Starbucks has great relationships with its partners and customers. It treats the coffee farmers honestly and fairly, and its accomplishments are mutually beneficial. The company has made major impacts on the communities it serves through support of community events, charitable programs, and volunteerism. But the key element that has skyrocketed Starbucks to be the exceptional company it is today is inventiveness. The company's originality sets the groundwork for its success in the future. Along with innovative programs and initiatives that have carved out their unique niche as the world's number one specialty coffee retailer, Starbucks knows—it's all in the beans.

Did You Know?

The coffee industry is responsible for 1,694,710 jobs in the United States for 2015.

Source: National Coffee Association.

The World's Best Coffee Beans

When people think of Starbucks, they think of superior quality. Starbucks coffee is the most recognized coffee brand around the world, and millions of people in roughly eighty countries know Starbucks as the world's finest coffee. The company purchases the best green beans (raw coffee beans that have not been roasted) in the world. The beans are the first step that differentiates this company from all others in the specialty coffee industry. In addition, it has developed exceptional expertise in roasting the beans.

A well-thought-out plan for selecting only the finest coffee beans illustrates Starbucks' passion for buying and roasting top-quality coffee. Starbucks purchases roughly 3 percent of coffee grown around the world, sourced from 400,000 farmers. As you can see from Table 8.1, coffee production is big business worldwide. The USDA forecasts world coffee production to be 169.1 million bags (60 kilograms/bag) for the 2019–2020 coffee year. Starbucks does not purchase the lower-quality robusta beans, even though these beans are cheaper. Finding the higher-quality arabica coffee beans, grown in distinct regions of the world, helps the company maintain its unique niche and has kept it ahead of its competition.

Coffee buyers for Starbucks travel the globe to purchase the premium coffee beans they demand. The evaluation process for choosing the beans includes roasting samples of coffee and taste-testing. This is a process called *cupping,* in which the aroma and aspects of taste (acidity, body, and flavor) are measured. Have you ever seen someone at a fancy restaurant savoring a sample of wine by holding it in her mouth for a few seconds to evaluate the bouquet and flavor? That is similar to cupping, but in this case, the commodity is coffee and the taste-testers are professionals. Only a very few of the tested coffee samples will make it to the Starbucks warehouses. While over seventy countries grow coffee, Starbucks purchases from just under 30 countries, heavily concentrated in Latin America, Africa, and Asia/Pacific. Even Hacienda Alsacia, Starbucks' own coffee farm located in Costa Rica, adds to the elite coffee supply. The farm was purchased in 2013 and serves as a global research and development facility for Starbucks.

Table 8.1   World Coffee Production for 2019–2020 (in 60 kg Bags)

Top Five Producers (forecast as of June 2019)	
Brazil	59.3 million
Vietnam	30.5 million
Columbia	14.3 million
Indonesia	10.7 million
Ethiopia	7.4 million
WORLD TOTAL	169.1 million

Source: Foreign Agricultural Service/USDA.

The purchased coffee beans are shipped fresh to one of five company roasting facilities, four located in the United States and one in Amsterdam. Starbucks roasters are experts at releasing the full flavor of the beans and are skilled in creating the signature Starbucks dark-roast flavor.

Starbucks is willing to pay top dollar for quality beans, too. In mid-2020, for example, world arabica prices were hovering above a dollar per pound. This is the "C" contract market price and is the worldwide trading reference utilized by coffee traders. By mid-2021 world arabica "C" prices had topped $1.30 per pound, but Starbucks has always, and still is, committed to paying more than the "C" price to compensate coffee farmers for maintaining premium quality. And while the "C" price tends to fluctuate due to speculation and annual weather conditions, the price Starbucks negotiates for its coffee tends to be relatively stable due to a large portion of fixed-price contracts (see the sidebar Coffee Talk interview with a spokesperson from ICE Futures U.S., to learn more about the "C" price). Starbucks buys its green coffee beans from exporters, farmers, farm cooperatives, and, on occasion, other importers.

Coffee Talk: *An Interview with a Spokesperson from the ICE Futures U.S. in New York*

The Coffee, Sugar, and Cocoa Exchange is now part of the Intercontinental Exchange (ICE) Futures U.S. in New York, as of 2007. It dates from 1882, when the Coffee Exchange of New York was established for merchants and traders. The coffee C Contract is the world benchmark market pricing for arabica coffee, and the coffee industry views the C Contract as a guide to the cost of business. Most coffee trades in the commodity market but Starbucks prefers to buy what it considers a high-quality grade directly from farmers.

The contract price includes physical delivery of the coffee, although it is largely used for hedging, with no physical delivery actually made. Only about 1 percent of transactions results in physical delivery from a supplier to a roaster or manufacturer. And you'd better know what you are buying, because if you do take delivery, a C Contract is for 37,500 pounds of coffee—enough to fill an entire truckload. Big companies that are highly competitive on price do buy here, trying to get coffee at the lowest price possible.

The Exchange uses select coffees from Mexico, El Salvador, Guatemala, Costa Rica, Nicaragua, Kenya, New Guinea, Panama, Tanzania, Uganda, Honduras, and Peru to establish the basis for the C Contract. Colombian coffee brings in a premium over the basis, and coffees judged of lesser quality from Venezuela, Burundi, India, Rwanda, the Dominican Republic, and Ecuador trade at a discount from the basis. Price differentials are determined based on the quality of beans, and traders buy and sell against those prices.

The contract prices physical delivery of exchange-grade green beans, from one of nineteen countries of origin. A price quote is listed, for example, at 136.20 cents per pound or $1.362 per pound. The C Contract is forced up or down due to supply-and-demand shifts, including unexpected weather conditions, such as a drought or flood; political turmoil or war; economic instability; and other unpredictable factors. Because Starbucks buys top-quality coffee, it typically pays a price above the C. But when the C skyrockets, so does the price of coffee for Starbucks. It is a basic economic indicator for the company.

The C Contract

Historically, weather fluctuations, long sea routes in trade, and imbalances of supply and demand caused huge variation in coffee pricing—so much so that in 1880, cash speculation in coffee caved the market. In an effort to bring some order to pricing in the coffee market, importers and dealers met in lower Manhattan on March 7, 1882, to trade in coffee futures. The first transaction on the New York Coffee Exchange was for 250 bags of coffee. A spokesperson from the ICE Futures U.S. in New York, where coffee is now traded, pointed out some of the details of trading this volatile commodity:

What is the Coffee C Contract? What is the contract size?

The contract calls for delivery of 37,500 pounds of arabica coffee in any one of several delivery points; full contract specifications are at https://www.theice.com/products/15

What percentage of traders actually take physical delivery of coffee?

Less than half of 1 percent of positions are held until the expiration of the futures contract and taken to delivery.

Why is there volatility in the coffee market?

As with other products, coffee prices are determined by supply-and-demand factors. Supply in particular is not constant, as the crop can be significantly increased by favorable weather and significantly decreased by unfavorable weather. This surely contributes to price volatility in the coffee market.

Explain what type of people (or businesses) might be interested in coffee contracts.

We generally divide traders of any of our products into two classes: *hedgers*, which in the coffee market would include producers, roasters, and merchant firms that help move the product from origin to end user and that therefore hold long inventories and also have sales commitments not offset by inventory held; and *speculators*, including individual speculators, funds, index investors, and so on.

Product Differentiation: More than the Coffee

The economic definition of *monopolistic competition* is a market structure in which many firms compete by selling a similar, but not identical, good or service. There are numerous firms in the industry in this market structure, and the barriers to entry into the market are low. In other words, the costs are relatively low to start up a coffeehouse, and many have attempted to enter the market. Once people see a good business opportunity, such as the coffeehouse phenomenon, many firms will enter the market in an attempt to make money. Many will fail, but some will succeed, and new entrants in the market will take some demand away from current producers in the market.

Starbucks is not a unique business; there are many firms running coffeehouses throughout the United States. There are thousands of smaller neighborhood coffee cafés, as well. And yes, Starbucks, Dunkin', and McDonald's are often referred to as the big three, due to intense competition. Starbucks' success has come from its expertise at product differentiation.

Starbucks has focused on taking an essentially similar retail good—coffee—and turning it into a unique product. The coffee, beverages, and food items that Starbucks sells are not identical to those at other coffeehouses. But besides differentiating its consumable products, it has also created a priceless intangible product over the years that hasn't been duplicated by others: the Starbucks Experience. Customers identify Starbucks with premium quality, serving the world's finest coffees in a friendly and welcoming setting. Starbucks coffeehouses also sell an elite dream, an atmosphere that can be a departure from real life, and a place for escape from the mundane.

Starbucks baristas boost this satisfying customer experience by adding education to each cup of coffee. By sharing information about the company's select coffees with patrons—from the qualities that make their flavors unique to their countries of origin—baristas help Starbucks customers become more knowledgeable about what they are drinking, feel good about the product, and become a part of the Starbucks coffee culture. The company is promoting its coffee products the way winemakers have long marketed wines, making the type of grapes and the area where it was grown important to the product.

Many competitors have tried to capitalize on the success of Starbucks and open their own upscale coffeehouses. Yet, the Starbucks Corporation has carved out a unique package that has been hard for others to duplicate. The company's retail coffeehouses become entwined with and support the communities in which they operate, and they develop a strong customer following. Starbucks customers are loyal and not likely to shift their preferences—each week, there are roughly 100 million unique visits to Starbucks. History has shown they have the power to raise prices without negative effect because of brand loyalty. The company has been ranked every year by *Forbes*, from 2013 to 2020, as one of the "World's Most Valuable Brands."

Competition Percolates

As consumers refine their taste for specialty coffee, major retail businesses have jumped into the gourmet market (see Table 8.2). Add a percolating economy to the increasing number of retail coffee sellers and it is an

Table 8.2 Comparing the Big Three

(year-end data, 2019 Annual Results)

	Dunkin'	*McDonald's*	*Starbucks*
Year founded	1950	1948	1971
Brand image	Modern	Convenience	High-end
Number of stores world	13,137	38,695	31,256
Global revenues	$672.8 million	$21.1 billion	$26.5 billion
Comp store sales	Int. 5.7% & United States 2.2%	Global 5.9%	Global 5.0%

all-out war to see who will make the most coffee cash. Starbucks may be the cream of the crop among retail coffeehouses, but it must keep its eyes open in this coffee conflict. Fast-food giant McDonald's has developed lower-priced tasty coffee treats, and donut ruler Dunkin' sells rich, premium arabica hot and cold brews. Starbucks should also have its eyes peeled on JAB Holding Co., a privately held German conglomerate that invests for the long-term in premium brands. JAB's vast holdings focus on consumer goods and consumer retail with one of the major interest areas, coffee, and JAB has lots of it. The company purchased a long-time Starbucks competitor, San Francisco-based Peet's Coffee & Tea in 2012, and Minneapolis's Caribou Coffee Company the same year and holds a host of other coffee businesses. Also serving coffee are some more of JAB's well-known holdings, Panera and Krispy Kreme.

Pivotal Places

Think you know a lot about the global coffee company? Match the place to the sentence for these important facts in Starbucks history:

CHOICES:

   Pike Place Market; Seattle; Japan; Costa Rica; Milan

1. Starbucks made its first endeavor into coffee research by purchasing its own coffee farm in 2013, Hacienda Alsacia, located in this country: _____
2. Starbucks' first international store was located in this country: _____
3. The original Starbucks store was located here: _____
4. Corporate headquarters and founding city of Starbucks: _____
5. After a business trip to this city, Howard Schultz was convinced the espresso café concept would be successful for Starbucks: _____

Answers: 1. Costa Rica; 2. Japan; 3. Pike Place Market; 4. Seattle; 5. Milan.

Dunkin'

When Dunkin' was founded in 1950, in Canton, Massachusetts, Dunkin' coffee was secondary to its outstanding baked goods. Previously known as Dunkin' Donuts, the company officially became Dunkin' in 2018. This company has long been known for donuts, but is now a powerhouse in the coffee arena as well. Dunkin', a destination for both high-quality coffee and donuts, bagels, breakfast sandwiches, and other baked goods, is under the parent company of Dunkin' Brands, along with Baskin-Robbins, the world's largest specialty ice cream retailer with thirty-one flavors of ice cream. Dunkin' has a total of 13,137 stores, 9,630 stores across the United States, in forty-three states, largely northeast, plus 3,507 international stores in fifty-one countries. Globally, it sells nearly 1.7 billion cups of hot and iced coffee each year.

Dunkin' stores are owned and operated exclusively by franchisees. Today, it offers ground and whole-bean coffee, espresso drinks, lattes, chilled drinks, frozen drinks, and more. In fiscal 2019, Dunkin' segments generated revenues of $672.8 million, or 51 percent of the total company segment revenues, of which $646.1 million attributed to the Dunkin' U.S. segment and $26.7 million was in the Dunkin' international segment. The modern update is expected to propel growth, the company noting in its 2019 annual report, "We believe that we have opportunities to continue to grow our Dunkin' and Baskin-Robbins concepts internationally in new and existing markets through brand and menu differentiation."

In 2018, Dunkin' had a remake; along with the name change, the company introduced a new store design. An aggressive media campaign touted the name change, along with the redo, to bring the seventy-year-old company into modern times. Stores are sleek and modern with updated décor, and so is Dunkin's new image. The company has been undergoing significant adjustment of its menu items. Donuts are still there but with a reduced selection, in favor of healthier options like egg and cheese on an English muffin, or twenty different vegan options.

Dunkin' features a mobile app, on-the-go ordering and pick-up, rewards program, and sandwiches throughout the day and in 2020 officially eliminated foam cups in favor of paper cups both nationally and internationally. A perusal through the company's website at www.dun kindonuts.com might remind you of Starbucks, but with a modern feel. The competition keeps getting stronger, while Dunkin' was long known as the second largest coffee chain it is now part of the second largest restaurant chain in the United States by sales and locations, behind McDonald's. On December 15, 2020, Inspire Brands, Inc. bought Dunkin' Brands Group (the parent company of Dunkin' and Baskin-Robbins) for $11.3 billion. Along with the Dunkin' and Baskin-Robbins, Inspire Brands owns Arby's Buffalo Wild Wings, SONIC Drive-In, Jimmy John's, and Rusty Taco. The acquisition by Inspire Brands allows Dunkin' to further benefit from economies of scale and team expertise. An Inspire Brands, Inc. press release dated, December 15, 2020, commented on the acquisition:

> Both Dunkin' and Baskin-Robbins will benefit by leveraging the capabilities and best practices of Inspire's shared services platform. Additionally, both brands will also benefit Inspire by adding a highly talented team, strong franchise network, large and loyal customer base, scaled international platform, as well as a robust consumer packaged goods licensing capability.

While the campaign continues for the coffee drinker's dollars, it's just another day at the shop for the giant Starbucks. It proves that coffee is indeed a tough business, but Starbucks has made it clear—it is in the game and here to stay.

McDonald's

Fast-food giant McDonald's, based in Oak Brook, Illinois, has been around since 1948, carrying the name of its founders, Dick and Mac McDonald. McDonald's Corporation operates 38,695 restaurants, of which 36,059 are franchised in 119 countries. It is one of the elite thirty stocks in the Dow Jones Industrial Average, a blue-chip stock that is an industry leader. And although the company has been fighting some financial struggles on the revenue side, their revenue number is still huge at $21.1 billion for fiscal 2019. Global comparable sales increased 5.9 percent across all industry segments for the same year, with comparable sales in the United States increasing 5.0 percent and comparable sales in the International Lead segment increasing a whopping 6.1 percent.

Along with traditional beverages, hamburgers, fries, breakfast meals, chicken nuggets and sandwiches, desserts, shakes, and salads, customers can enjoy a wide variety of coffee delectable. The fast-food giant entered the specialty coffee arena in 2009 in the United States with a few basic offerings, but today McDonald's McCafe beverage line, offering café-style drinks, is explosive. As of early 2021, the McCafe line was offering twenty-five coffee-based drinks, such as Iced French Vanilla Coffee, Carmel Latte, Mocha, or an Americano (which is hot water poured over espresso). Check out the current menu on www.mcdonalds.com. Unlike Starbucks, McDonald's does not roast its own beans, but purchases the coffee from a select group of roasters, utilizing only arabica beans, like Starbucks. The main difference on the coffee front is price. McDonald's McCafe drinks are noticeably lower in price than Starbucks coffee. As a matter of fact, a small hot coffee at McDonald's is still just a $1.00.

Mickey D's, as the company is sometimes informally called, is known for convenience and a value-priced menu. In order to keep up with the times and combat slumping revenue, the company launched a growth plan to include emphasis on modern technologies to enhance the restaurant experience. A global mobile app, digital menu boards, and self-order kiosks were at the core of the technology upgrade. Many McDonald's restaurants currently offer the self-ordering kiosk where customers can customize and pay for their orders, increasing convenience and speed for customers. Struggling through slumped sales during the COVID-19 pandemic the in-store kiosk allows customers to pick up orders without ever coming in contact with an employee. But it's not just about speed, the company is mindful, too, of menu innovations and healthier options. Often known as a fast-food unhealthy dining option, along with the vast array of coffee drinks, the company has attempted to appeal to the health trend. You can now find fruit smoothies, egg McMuffins, whole-grain oatmeal, to name just a few healthy treats. A fun fact about Happy Meals, according to McDonald's website: "We began evolving the Happy Meal in the U.S. in 2004, when we started offering choices such as Apple Dippers, milk and apple juice in select markets. In 2012, we began automatically including Apple Slices in every Happy Meal."

Who will be the winner of the coffee conflict? Starbucks wins on premium sourcing, taste, and an upscale environment. But when another downturn in the economy hits, watch some Starbucks loyalists flock to McDonald's to enjoy café-style coffee at a budget price. And for customers craving a donut, Dunkin' is the obvious choice, accompanied by a great tasting cup of coffee, of course.

Multinational Competition

If you have not heard of U.K.-based Costa Coffee, you will very soon. The world's largest beverage company, Coca-Cola, acquired Costa for $4.9 billion in early 2019. Costa is the largest British coffee establishment with roughly 2,700 coffee shops in the United Kingdom and is a leading international company. Costa has over 3,800 stores across the globe in forty-one countries, and with the newly earned distribution channels and economies of scale of the $221 billion market cap Coca-Cola, this coffee chain has the capability of being a significant global competitor.

Costa Coffee roasts its own beans, has a mobile app, sells bagged coffee, and has retail coffeehouses. Sounds familiar, Starbucks? Two notable items for Costa, which carries an original blend of delicate arabica and strong robusta beans: (1) many of its locations are self-serve coffee bars, aka vending machines, and (2) following the acquisition by Coca-Cola, the company launched a new line of chilled Costa Coffee ready-to-drink products in Britain. At the time of this writing, there were no brick-and-mortar Costa shops in the United States, but in 2020 the company opened fifty self-serve kiosks throughout America. International market competition could be serious for Starbucks. Keeping no secrets, a press release from Coca-Cola announcing the acquisition ("The Coca-Cola Company to Acquire Costa," August 31, 2018) hints at a heavy move into China, Starbucks' hottest area for growth. "For Coca-Cola, the expected acquisition adds a scalable coffee platform with critical know-how and expertise in a fast-growing, on-trend category. Costa ranks as the leading coffee company in the United Kingdom and has a growing footprint in China, among other markets."

CEO Kevin Johnson has been very open about his vision for China. For Starbucks, China is the fastest growing market and the second largest market overall. The company currently has a reported 4,704 stores in China, along with its Shanghai Roastery, opened in 2017. But the Chinese coffee market may be up for grabs. Yet another company, Luckin Coffee, was a fast growing competitor in China. Founded in 2017 with one Beijing location and headquartered in Xiamen, China, Luckin is a technology-driven coffeehouse, serving arabica coffee. The company became a publicly traded company on NASDAQ in 2019, opening up its opportunities for funding, and quickly raised nearly $900 million from investors. A scandal in 2019 where Luckin reportedly intentionally fabricated sales of $300 million sent shares plummeting and caused NASDAQ to delist the stock.

The jury is out if Luckin is still a viable competitor. According to its prospectus, within eighteen months of opening its first Beijing store, the company had 2,370 stores in twenty-eight cities in China. Technology is the key to this cashless store; all purchases are made via Luckin's mobile app. Focusing on efficiency, over 90 percent of the stores are referred to as pick-up stores, with limited seating available. The remainder of stores are called relax stores; this is a traditional-type coffeehouse, with delivery kitchens (only serving delivery orders). Luckin Coffee had ambitious plans to dominate coffee in China and states this goal in its prospectus:

China's coffee market is highly underpenetrated. Inconsistent qualities, high prices and inconvenience have hampered the growth of the freshly brewed coffee market in China. We believe that our model has successfully driven the mass market coffee consumption in China by addressing these pain points. We aim to become the largest coffee network in China, in terms of number of stores, by the end of 2019.

Luckin reportedly is operating 4,507 stores in China across more than forty cities. The company now trades as an over-the-counter (OTC) stock and while it has dipped significantly from its highs in early 2020, the company maintains it will be a contender. On December 16, 2020, the company agreed to settle with the Securities and Exchange Commission with a $180 million fine in penalties associated with the fraud. A Luckin press release dated January 7, 2021, noted:

> The Company's new leadership team has developed an updated business plan that has resulted in top line and store profitability growth in 2020, overcoming significant financial and operational challenges. Luckin Coffee's positive momentum continues under the new management team, with 35.8% year-over-year net revenue growth in the third quarter of 2020 and over 60% of stores achieving positive profitability in November 2020.

There are many heavy hitters in the international java market: Dunkin', McDonald's, JAB Holding, Costa Coffee, and possibly Luckin Coffee. Although the gloves have come off, Starbucks seems to be taking it all in stride.

What Is Coffee Cupping?

Coffee cupping is a method of evaluating the aroma and taste of brewed coffee. It is generally employed by professionals in the trade to evaluate the quality of a coffee bean, but cupping can be practiced by anyone to get an understanding of different coffee regions. Cupping requires first sniffing the coffee, then drawing a sip of the coffee to the roof of the month so it spreads to the back of the tongue, and finally rolling the coffee around in the mouth to begin to identify distinctive flavors and where it was grown. Most people then spit out the coffee.

Ask yourself, "Is it a full-bodied coffee?" and "Does it taste bitter?" Use statements like, "The aroma is fruity" or "What a spicy aroma," and you will fit right in with the pros. See if you can pick out the traits that are unique to coffees from different regions. What makes a coffee from Costa Rica different from an Ethiopian-grown coffee? Comparing and contrasting coffees allows you to develop an appreciation of different coffees and their specific tastes. And although cuppers, as they are called, definitely have a unique professional skill, personal opinion comes into play.

According to the Specialty Coffee Association (SCA), a cupper generally looks at these six characteristics:

- Fragrance—the smell of beans after grinding
- Aroma—the smell of ground-up beans after they are steeped in water
- Taste—the flavor of the coffee
- Nose—the vapors released by the coffee in the mouth
- Aftertaste—the vapors and flavors that remain after swallowing
- Body—the feel of the coffee in the mouth

Why not try your hand at cupping? Coffee tasting can be an interesting experience, so go ahead and prepare a simple coffee cupping for your favorite adult coffee drinkers—parents, relatives, or family friends. You should have no trouble finding willing participants. Comparing various brewed coffees can help one decide which bean is most to one's liking.

Keep it simple and start with just a few coffee varieties. Be sure to brew the coffee fresh. The samples should be small, and two fresh cups should be available for each coffee. A large spoon helps in the tasting. And, of course, make sure you have written down descriptions of your coffees to share with the taste testers, aka the cuppers, when they are done choosing their favorites. Provide evaluation forms for the individuals to write down descriptive comments about each coffee. To increase their coffee IQ, at the end of the cupping you can reveal the descriptions of the coffees and let each participant guess the origin of the coffee brews. The adults may enjoy the experience so much, they will want to have a formal coffee tasting party for their friends. Over 60 percent of Americans consume coffee on a regular basis, so a coffee party is likely going to be a popular event.

Coffee Talk: *A Chat with Ted Lingle on Coffee Industry Trends*

Ted Lingle has an expansive wealth of knowledge about the coffee industry, with over fifty years of experience in the business. Since 2006, he has been the executive director of the Coffee Quality Institute (CQI), an organization he cofounded with the goal of creating a sustainable supply of quality coffee for the industry. Previously, Lingle served as executive director of the Specialty Coffee Association of America (SCAA). He is the author of *The Coffee Cupper's Handbook* (2008) and *The Coffee Brewing Handbook* (1996). Lingle was a founding cochairman of the SCAA and has also participated on committees for the National Coffee Association and National Coffee Service Association. In addition, he has served as chairman of the board of directors of the Coffee Development Group/Promotion Fund of the ICO.

He began his coffee career in 1970, when he was employed as vice president of marketing for Lingle Bros. Coffee, Inc. For twenty years he coordinated the sales and marketing activities of a prominent coffee roaster in Southern California. For the past five years he has served as the senior advisor to the Yunnan International Coffee Exchange, located in China, assisting them to introduce Chinese coffees into the specialty coffee market. The coffee expert answered some pointed questions on coffee consumption, supply-and-demand instabilities, and industry trends:

What is the Coffee Quality Institute?

The Coffee Quality Institute (CQI) is a nonprofit association that was started in 1995. It is a 501(c)(3) foundation formed to improve the quality of coffee and the lives of the people that produce it. Much of our work is funded by USAID (U.S. Agency for International Development), our largest funding source.

How much coffee is consumed worldwide each year?

Coffee is one of the most widely traded commodities in the world, with an industry employing over 130 million people worldwide. The world is currently consuming all the coffee it is producing. This comes to roughly 150 million bags of coffee a year. Each bag is 60 kilos, or 132 pounds.

How has per capita consumption changed over the years?

Per capita consumption in the United States went from 7 kilos per person down to 3 kilos per person in a 30-year period, from 1962 to 1992. The primary reason was that in the 1960s, there was a downturn in the blend quality from the major roasters. Roasters started using the cheaper Robusta blends, indirectly driving consumption down. Robusta has double the caffeine and a more bitter taste. Consumers responded appropriately by migrating to other beverages.

How has the growth of coffeehouses changed coffee habits?

The trend started in the early 1960s that caused a paradigm shift. During that time, consumers began to realize there were major quality and taste differences in coffees. It changed their attitudes and behavior when it came to coffee purchasing. Consumers who would pay $4 for a pound of Folgers became comfortable paying $15 for a pound of Starbucks.

How do demand and supply instabilities affect the price of coffee?

Beginning in the 1990s, a new country—Vietnam—jumped into the coffee market. While initially Vietnam produced 500,000 bags a year, in 2000, it had jumped to 15 million bags. Vietnam is now the second-leading coffee-producing country (after Brazil), producing low-grade Robusta coffees. The prices were so low that many roasters have moved from higher-quality Central American Arabica coffee to purchase from Vietnam.

But the market is really a two-tiered market based on quality. People can perceive quality taste differences, and caffeine content causes consumers to self-regulate. Robusta contains twice the caffeine of Arabica, causing those who don't easily metabolize caffeine to reduce consumption. The lower quality Robusta coffees will continue to have lower prices due to increases in supply.

What type of impact has Starbucks made on the coffee industry?

The industry was alive and well before Starbucks. The people who started Starbucks learned from Alfred Peet. He was one of the individuals who were developing the specialty coffee market in the 1960s and helped create the explosion for the market in the 1990s.

Starbucks was in the right place at the right time. Starbucks was one of the stock-market darlings of the 1990s, with a highly successful initial public offering (IPO). Starbucks has brought high visibility to the consumer. It has dramatically expanded convenience reach for the consumer, making coffee a beverage of choice. It is no longer, "Do I want a cup of coffee?" but, "What kind of coffee do I want? An espresso, latté, or chilled cappuccino?"

Starbucks represents only one in four coffee stores, and one-half of the stores are independent businesses. Specialty coffee represents a business opportunity for an entrepreneur to risk it all and to take a chance to open the doors to a great business. It is the entrepreneurial spirit that drives Americans to start a business. The coffeehouse is a great model.

What continues to drive specialty coffee consumption?

In the last decade the greatest change in consumption has been the continued rapid growth of cold coffee beverages, from ice-blended coffee drinks served in coffee cafes to the RTD (ready-to-drink) beverages sold in supermarkets and convenience stores. Today, the newest innovation is the "nitro-brew" cold coffee beverage found in many high-end cafes. As predicted, within the next decade, cold coffee beverages will outsell hot coffee beverages in the United States. Starbucks continues to be an industry leader in offering a wide variety of cold coffee beverages.

How has digital innovation and technology changed the coffee business?

Digital innovation and technology have led to major improvements in all types of coffee processing equipment, from coffee roasters to coffee brewers. Small, in-store roasting machines now have the capability of computerized roaster controls originally found only on large industrial-sized roasters. The same miniaturization has aided the development of the immensely popular single-cup brewers.

Do you think the coffee competition in China will have an impact on Starbucks?

Southeast Asia, especially China, is becoming the new "center of gravity" for the specialty coffee industry, for both production and consumption. China, like Brazil, India and Ethiopia, will become both a major consumer and producer of coffee. My prediction is that within the next two decades, China will become the world's seventh largest producer of Arabica coffees and the world's third largest coffee consuming nation; first will be Brazil, second will be the United States, and third will be China. Starbucks has come to the same conclusion and is now actively buying green coffees grown in Yunnan Province in China and aggressively competing for retail space in this newly emerging market.

CHAPTER NINE

Coping with Controversy

At every turn, let us choose to replace meanness with kindness; pettiness with significance; hate with love; gridlock with compromise; complaints with creative solutions.

—Howard Schultz, Chairman Emeritus Starbucks,
*From the Ground Up: A Journey to Reimagine the
Promise of America* (2019)

Starbucks has certainly had its share of troubles and even tragedy in recent years. Underperforming stores and market saturation have been coupled with coffee competition in domestic and foreign markets, including China, Starbucks rising star. The company's revenue for health is less robust than before and to top it off, the company's guru, Howard Schultz, retired and stepped down from day-to-day operations. The company has suffered from some criticism and bad press recently. Some of the less-flattering critiques claim Starbucks has a racial bias problem; it doesn't play fair with employee rights; the company is trying to destroy Christmas; the company avoids taxes in the United Kingdom; and, a sore point for the environmentally concerned, the new sippy cup lids contain more plastic than the old straw/cup combination. Let us explore and get to the root of these issues.

Did You Know?

If you have ever had your name spelled incorrectly on a Starbucks cup, don't feel bad. It happens to celebrities, too. On recent outings to the coffeehouse, actress Reese (Witherspoon) was spelled Greece, basketball star Dwayne (Wade) was spelled Dane, and soccer champ Carli (Lloyd) was spelled Nardley. Mega-star Oprah was not even recognized on a recent Starbucks run. After divulging her name as Oprah, the barista added insult to injury by asking her how to spell her name.

Source: Kate Hogan, "Oprah Winfrey, Michael Phelps and More Stars Who Have Had Their Names Hilariously Misspelled on Coffee Cups," People.com, March 1, 2018.

Labor Complaints and Union Struggles

Starbucks employees—or partners, as they are called—have always been an important part of the company. The coffee giant touts itself as the socially responsible company. Starbucks has always made it a point to provide great benefits to partners—health insurance for full- and part-time employees; college tuition assistance; parental leave; a 401k plan; Bean Stock that permits partial ownership of the company; and a free 1-pound bag of coffee each week. Although labor unions at Starbucks are rare, in 2004, the first Starbucks employee union was formed to advocate for improving conditions in the work environment.

The Starbucks Workers Union (SWU) was formed to organize the retail employees of Starbucks. Some of the more vocal complaints from partners involve bad hours, low pay, and insurance they can't afford. The SWU members are interested in strong wage strength, working hours, and job climate. SWU is a part of the Industrial Workers of the World (IWW) union. The IWW has a long history that dates back to the early 1900s. So far, the SWU has had some success at recruitment, mainly in the states of New York, Michigan, Minnesota, Illinois, and even in Quebec City. On Twitter (Starbucks Union@starbucksunion) they specifically state its purpose: "A grassroots union of over 300 baristas united for a living wage, secure work hours, and systemic change at the world's largest coffee chain."

The National Labor Relations Board (NLRB), an independent federal agency created by Congress to administer the National Labor Relations Act, was designed to safeguard employees' rights to organize and to remedy unfair labor practices. The IWW has a long list of charges against Starbucks claiming, among other things, discriminatory treatment of pro-union workers. The list includes such concerns as terminations for union support, prohibiting employees from union discussions, and interrogating employees about their support of a union. The legal wrangling between the NLRB and Starbucks continues and has been plentiful through the years, but the year 2009 brought a major settlement, the sixth in three years. According to a Wolters Kluwer report dated June 9, 2009

("Starbucks settles with NLRB over unfair labor practices"), the terms Starbucks agreed to in order to remedy the alleged violations include "Reinstatement of IWW members who were charged for their union activity" and "Invalidation of Starbucks' national policy that prohibited employees from sharing written union information and joining the union on company property."

In his 1997 book about Starbucks, Schultz writes about the care with which he believes employees should be treated. Clearly, he believes he treats his employees well. "If there's one accomplishment I'm proudest of at Starbucks, it's the relationship of trust and confidence we've built with the people who work at the company. That's not just an empty phrase, as it is with so many companies," Schultz wrote (Schultz and Yang 1997, 6). "We treat warehouse workers and entry-level retail people with the kind of respect that most companies show for only high executives."

In fact, in an August 8, 2006, press release fact sheet, Starbucks strongly states its position on union representation of partners:

> Starbucks firmly believes that the direct employment relationship which we currently have with our partners is the best way to help ensure a great work environment. We believe we do not need a third party to act on behalf of our partners. We prefer to deal directly with them in a fair and respectful manner, just as we have throughout our history.

The SWU is not the only union that has had issues with the company. The International Union of Operating Engineers Local 286 had a disagreement with Starbucks. It used to represent Starbucks' maintenance mechanics and technicians at the company's Kent, Washington, roasting plant. The union no longer represents the workers, but in 2005, Starbucks settled charges the union had filed with the NLRB, accusing the company of systematically screening out job applicants who had previously worked at unionized employers or had other perceived union sympathies. In 2005, Starbucks paid out $165,000 to eight employees of this facility to settle charges that they had been retaliated against for being pro-union. Starbucks was accused of screening out individuals who had any pro-union connections. The charge also said the company dismissed an employee because he would not discontinue this practice. The company did not admit to any wrongdoing. However, it did agree to pay the employee $125,000 and to pay $5,000 and offer employment to each of eight individuals who had earlier been turned down for jobs.

While the NLRB is certainly keeping busy investigating complaints against the company, a digital platform entered the arena and has absorbed labor complaints and issues. Coworker.org is a digital tool for workers to express and share their concerns, an online platform founded in 2013. According to their website, this nonprofit organization fiscally sponsored by the New Venture Fund is "developing digital infrastructure for a labor movement of the 21st century—networked, global, and powered by data, technology, and the leadership of workers in every workplace." As of this writing, Coworker.org tallies 43,143 people who indicate they work at Starbucks and are using the network. Workers can join an employee network for support or comments or start a campaign.

The Starbucks campaigns on Coworker.org are plentiful, but notable petitions include barista Kristie Williams' August 2014 petition to change the dress code to allow visible tattoos at the company. Over 25,000 signatures quickly flooded the petition. Was Starbucks listening? Likely, because in October 2014, Starbucks announced its new dress code which includes allowing employees to display their tattoos (just not on the face or neck). The biggest petition noticed by Starbucks was the 2016 petition by barista Jaime Prater, "Starbucks, Lack of Labor Is Killing Morale." Prater speaks of extreme labor cuts and understaffed stores, "Baristas also continue to struggle in their stores, with more expectation, with less support staff." Howard Schultz even phoned Prater for a chat to better understand his concerns and issues. To date, the petition carries 20,765 signatures but it was not until 2018 that baristas were given a pay boost and increased benefits.

Starbucks reports a partner count of 228,000 people in the United States, roughly 220,000 in company-operated stores and the others working in corporate, store development, roasting, manufacturing, warehousing, and distribution, with a long record of employee support and social responsibility. For a company that claims to value its partners, any hint of unfair labor practices or disgruntled masses is surely unwanted press. The company is no doubt mindful of these labor issues.

Did You Know?

How many Starbucks are there in the world? 32,660

In March 2019, Starbucks opened its 30,000th store in Shenzhen, China.

Source: Starbucks 10-K 2020 and Q2 Fiscal 2020 Results.

Critics Slam Ethos

Ethos Water is a bottled water with a social mission of helping children get clean water. The Ethos brand emerged from an idea Peter Thum developed after working on a consulting project in South Africa. The strategy consultant noticed that many people there did not have access to clean drinking water. After researching this problem around the world and consulting on a project in the bottled-water industry, he realized there was an opportunity to create a new bottled-water brand that could help children and their communities have access to safe water through its sales. In 2002, Thum left his job to envision and develop Ethos Water; he brought in friend and business school roommate Jonathan Greenblatt a year later to be his partner. Thum and Greenblatt founded Ethos Water in 2003.

Thum and Greenblatt self-funded the launch of Ethos and even made the first deliveries out of an old Volvo station wagon. For every bottle of water that sells, 5 cents was donated toward solving the world water crisis. But now, the vision has been taken to a whole new level. Ethos Water was acquired by Starbucks in 2005 for $7.7 million, giving the bottled-water company a much larger distribution channel. What is unique about their company is that a percentage of its profits go to support clean-water programs in developing countries, including Tanzania, Indonesia, Columbia, Guatemala, and Nicaragua. The contribution to humanitarian efforts of giving 5 cents from every bottle purchased to the Ethos Water Fund, part of the Starbucks Foundation, is a practice continued by Starbucks.

Since 2005, $13.8 million has been granted through the Ethos Water Fund to aid water, sanitation, and hygiene education programs and benefiting more than 500,000 people globally. Each upscale bottle—attractive and relatively expensive—roughly $2.25 for a 23.7-ounce bottle—raises awareness of the world water crisis for those who read the print embossed on the plastic. It may make some customers feel good; not only do they quench their thirst when they buy this water, but they help fund clean-water projects in struggling countries around the world.

The name Ethos is even derived from the Greek *ethos,* meaning the distinguishing character, sentiment, moral nature, or guiding beliefs of a person, group, or institution. The slang reference to the water calls it ethics in a bottle. Let us investigate the issues surrounding the clean-water company.

Each bottle states that 5 cents from its sale will be donated to fund humanitarian water programs. Proponents may say this is one quick and easy way for the typical consumer to practice social responsibility. Of course, those who have had an introductory economics class will also realize that Ethos Water creates jobs. Employment is good for the economy and gets money circulating through the system, but the controversy is multifold. Some people think that by selling Ethos Water, Starbucks is cashing in on a humanitarian effort.

Critics claim Ethos Water is a way for the company to profit, and more should be donated to aid. The 5 cents per bottle is not significant enough. Others argue that buying water is not a good use of consumer funds— instead, they say, fill up a thermos with tap water and donate the entire $2.25 you would pay for the bottled water. There is one more point of contention: Even though recycling is one of Starbucks' mantras, everyone knows that not all the bottles will be recycled; some will go to landfills. To fuel the fire even further, in 2015 when the drought hit California and water conservation efforts were underway, Starbucks was still sourcing Ethos Water from a private spring in Merced, California. Starbucks did respond to the drought situation by moving the natural springs source and manufacturing out of the drought-stricken state of California to Pennsylvania, but not before incriminating press articles hit the news media.

Ethos promotes a social mission to help bring clean water to many people, but it may be adding to the world's plastic pollution problem. There are undoubtedly some Ethos bottles lying around in landfills. It might be better to enjoy tap water and reduce the plastic in our environment. It seems counterintuitive to help children in other countries, but create more waste and pollution here at home. It's certainly a social dilemma. What do you think? Is this a wonderful business idea that raises money for the sorely needed water projects in underdeveloped countries? Or is it simply another way for Starbucks to make a profit?

Did You Know?

Growth in coffee production rose substantially in 2017–2018, to 163.51 million bags, 4.8 percent higher than in 2016–2017. What is the official measurement of each bag? 132.276 pounds of coffee.

Source: International Coffee Organization, Annual Review 2017–18.

Recyclable Lid Is Criticized

Apart from the Ethos plastic water bottle controversy, Starbucks largely gets high marks for its environmental-friendly focus. In fact, Starbucks is a founding member, along with McDonald's, of the NextGen Cup

Challenge, an open competitive initiative to help end cup waste globally. The coffee company's environmental goals are lofty. By 2020, Starbucks says it will eliminate single-use plastic straws and will use their new strawless lid for its drinks, and herein lies the criticism. The strawless lids (yes, some people refer to them as adult sippy cups) were implemented in all stores in the United States and Canada in 2019 and will be used by more than 30,000 stores worldwide in 2020, eliminating more than 1 billion straws a year. The reason for the change is because straws can end up in the ocean and endanger the sea turtle by becoming stuck in its naval cavity and throat, and most of the plastic straws end up in landfills.

Is it a good idea? Most people say yes because they are small, therefore no recycle markings or instructions are on them, and most people just toss them in the trash. Okay, so far this sure doesn't sound like an environmental problem, but there is more to the story. A multitude of writers and environmentalists could not wait to get their scales out and try to compare the plastic used in the old lid/straw combination to the weight measurements provided by Starbucks for the new strawless lid. The media stories came out that the new lid used more plastic than the old lid/straw combo, and because much of the material ends up in landfills, the weight of the plastic should be a concern to environmentalists. After much hype and bad press, how much more plastic actually is in the new lid? Less. Starbucks clarified in a recent press release dated March 20, 2019, "The new lids have 9% less plastic than the current lid and straw." Still, the seed of possible environmental unfriendliness from the company had been planted.

Remember, if you want to help in the pursuit of a greener world, Starbucks gives a 10-cent discount when customers bring their own reusable cups. And if you stay in the store to drink your coffee, be sure to ask for a ceramic "for here" mug, which can be provided by the coffeehouse.

Closing Stores and Layoffs

Trying to make the right business moves and shore up excesses does not necessarily make for good publicity. This was certainly solidified following an investor announcement on June 19, 2018 ("Starbucks to Close 150 Stores"). Although a fairly detailed press release, the news media and public focused on the announced closing of 150 underperforming company-operated stores in the United States during fiscal year 2019 (ending September 30). Why big news? This was a triple-threat plan as Starbucks historically closes about fifty stores annually. Starbucks shared with investors that it anticipated same-store sales globally to grow just

1 percent in the third quarter of fiscal year 2018. Same-store sales or comparable-store sales is a key measurement in financial analysis, measuring revenue generated by stores in a particular period, compared to a similar period in the past. (Update: Global same-store sales growth did rise to 1 percent in the third quarter of fiscal 2018 and the company closed a total of 196 U.S. company-operated stores in fiscal 2019.)

An action plan to close the underperforming stores would no doubt assist in tackling the low growth rate. Other steps included major digital initiatives designed to contribute to comparable sales growth in the United States by 1–2 percent, partnering with an external consultant to identify areas of opportunity, and even accelerating a return of cash to shareholders beginning with an approved 20 percent increase in the quarterly dividend. Still, shareholders were not pleased. Following an explanatory Oppenheimer conference that afternoon by Kevin Johnson, Starbucks President and CEO, and Scott Maw, Starbucks CFO, the stock hit came the next day.

The Starbucks store closures were a hot news topic for a two-day period, leading to much speculation and opinion on the company's health in those 24-hour news cycles. Big news agencies led the press with headlines like "Starbucks to Close 150 Stores," and broadcasters ran leads, "Starbucks Shares Fall on Weak Forecasts." The next morning, Johnson appeared on CNBC's *Squawk on the Street* addressing the company's recent slowdown and growth plans. Johnson, characteristically upbeat, explained their growth had slowed in the last two or three years and recently announced plans were to close 150 stores in underperforming markets; but the company still planned to open 400 new stores in the United States.

Starbucks stock opened the market on June 20 at a respectable $54.83 but, after the announcement gained exposure, nose-dived to close at $52.22. In addition to the deep dive, heavy trading volume of 61,878,900 shares was seen that day, over six times the trading volume of 9,965,500 the day of the announcement. This significant trading volume and price decrease hinted at investor skepticism, dumping stock, and certainly a negative sign. The news media spoke and so did investors.

Arrest at Philadelphia Starbucks

On the eve of April 12, 2018, two African American men arrived early at a Starbucks in Philadelphia for a real estate meeting. They did not make a purchase, but sat down at a table, waiting for another individual to arrive. The two were having a real estate meeting with a developer. When one asked to use the restroom, they were told it was only for paying customers. An employee then told the men to make a purchase or leave. The men did not buy anything and within minutes the Starbucks manager called 911, stating, "I have two gentlemen in my café that are refusing to make a purchase or leave." The police arrived, arrested, and handcuffed the two men, and the arrest was captured on video by another customer. The video was immediately shared online and picked up by the news media, drawing outrage, protests, and accusations of racial discrimination. The men spent nearly nine hours in jail before being released, and no charges were filed.

The Starbucks company issued an initial press release saying, "We apologize to the two individuals and our customers and are disappointed this led to an arrest" ("Starbucks Response to Incident in Our Philadelphia Store," April 14, 2018). CEO and President Kevin Johnson took personal accountability for the situation, calling the incident a reprehensible outcome. In a letter to Starbucks partners and customers the leader wrote:

> First, to once again express our deepest apologies to the two men who were arrested with a goal of doing whatever we can to make things right. Second, to let you know of our plans to investigate the pertinent facts and make any necessary changes to our practices that would help prevent such an occurrence from ever happening again. And third, to reassure you that Starbucks stands firmly against discrimination or racial profiling.
> ("Starbucks CEO: Reprehensible Outcome in Philadelphia Incident," April 15, 2018)

On April 16, 2018, Johnson posted a follow-up video on the Starbucks Stories website. "I will fix this," Johnson said, again stressing personal responsibility for the situation. He explained the gentlemen did not deserve what happened to them and he would ensure that this is fixed and would never happen again. He explained that necessary changes to company practices would be forthcoming. The video concluded with the words, "We will address this, and we will be a better company" ("Video: A Follow-Up Message from Starbucks CEO in Philadelphia").

Members from the leadership team spent time in Philadelphia, and after much productive conversation, including Johnson speaking with the two gentlemen at the center of the discussion, a plan of action was quickly taken by the company. On May 29, 2018, for 4 hours in the afternoon, the company closed more than 8,000 company-owned U.S. stores and provided mandatory antibias training to 175,000 partners. Starbucks consulted with a multitude of individuals to develop the training curriculum, including award-winning documentary film maker, Stanley Nelson, who created a near 8-minute-long film about racial bias and the history of African Americans' access to public spaces for the training. Starbucks noted that the training will not stop after only that one day, with more training to come. This "disheartening incident," in the words of Johnson, has triggered the Third Place Policy, meaning any customer is welcome to use Starbucks spaces, even if they have not made a purchase at the store. This means all customers, purchasing and nonpurchasing, are welcome to use the restrooms and meet in stores.

Bad Press on Minimal Tax Payment

For Starbucks, the bad press regarding Starbucks' tax payments started in October 2012 in the United Kingdom. The headlines in a London *Reuters* article (Bergin, T., dated October 15, 2012) read "Special Report: How Starbucks Avoids U.K. Taxes," followed by many articles and news reports. Although all news agencies noted that Starbucks did nothing illegal, the company still faced backlash for its low tax bill. Writer Tom Bergin notes, "Accounts filed by its U.K. subsidiary show that since it opened in the U.K. in 1998, the company has racked up over 3 billion pounds ($4.8 billion) in coffee sales, and opened 735 outlets but paid only 8.6 million pounds in income taxes." The article speculated on the legal strategies the company was utilizing—intellectual property tax havens, transfer prices for goods that pass through different group entities, and intercompany loans.

Starbucks is aware that the perception as a tax avoider has lingered with the U.K. public through the years. In 2014 the company moved its regional headquarters from Amsterdam to London, and tax payments did rise. When an article ran in the *Financial Times* (Marriage, M., September 18, 2018) titled "Starbucks' European Unit Paid 2.8% U.K. Tax Last Year," Martin Brok, President Starbucks Europe, Middle East and Africa (EMEA), was quick to respond in a letter sent to the editors of the *Financial Times*. Brok noted that he wanted to clear up any false impressions due to the fact that the *Financial Times* reported on only two of the U.K. entities that exist. Brok continued, "As our public filings clearly show, there are now five Starbucks companies headquartered in the U.K. since we moved our regional headquarters here several years ago. The effective rate of corporation tax paid by these U.K. businesses to the British exchequer is 25.3%—substantially more than the U.K.'s corporation tax rate of 19.5%." The letter concludes, "We would hope that the *Financial Times* will report our tax affairs accurately in the future." Not only is Starbucks paying more taxes in the United Kingdom, but the company is clearly on the PR bandwagon.

California Cancer Ruling on Coffee

To understand the California cancer coffee ruling debacle, one must undergo a bit of coffee education and then follow the legal trail. At the center of the issue is acrylamide, a chemical that forms in certain foods during high-temperature processes such as banking, frying, or roasting. When coffee beans are roasted, acrylamide is released, so extremely minute amount of the chemical is present in coffee.

In 2010, the Council of Education and Research on Toxics (CERT), a California public benefit corporation, brought a lawsuit against Starbucks and over ninety other coffee companies to reduce the amount of acrylamide levels in coffee. The lawsuit was initiated under California's Proposition 65, officially known as the Safe Drinking Water and Toxic Enforcement Act of 1986. Prop 65 requires the state to keep an updated list of chemicals identified as causing cancer or reproductive toxicity. Businesses must post warning labels to Californians about significant exposures to these chemicals, enabling individuals to make informed decisions. Acrylamide is on the Prop 65 list.

Despite the overwhelming amount of research that indicates coffee is not cancer causing, in March 2018, a Los Angeles judge ruled that coffee must have a warning label. The President and CEO of the National Coffee Association, William Murray, writes, "These labels and signs have confused consumers—for good reason. The very idea of 'cancer warnings' for coffee contradicts the real-world evidence." Murray continues, "The total body of research regarding coffee was reviewed recently by the World Health Organization, which concluded that coffee is not carcinogenic and may even help protect against some types of cancer" (Murray, W., NCA in the News: "Prop 65: Coffee Gets the All Clear in California," June 3, 2019). Starbucks and other companies argued that acrylamide posed no significant risk in coffee and stressed the positive health benefits of the beverage. The final conclusion was that California's Office of Environmental Health Hazard Assessment, in June 2019, decided the acrylamide dose in coffee is too low to be a carcinogenic risk; the state regulator exempted coffee from the rule requiring warning labels. After all the controversy, there would be no cancer warning labels required on coffee sold in California. This debacle was not only controversial but confusing to consumers as well.

Ariana Grande Nonvegan Starbucks Drink

In 2019, Ariana Grande helped Starbucks launch a new drink, Cloud Macchiato. After tweeting a series of cloud teasers, finally on March 5, 2019, the collaboration between Starbucks and Grande became apparent. In a Starbucks Stories release from March 5, 2019 ("You'll Be on Cloud 9 with the Newest Starbucks Beverage"), Heidi Peiper described the drink, "Available in two flavors, caramel and cinnamon, Starbucks Cloud Macchiato beverages feature whipped cold milk foam that has a light, fluffy and silky-smooth texture." Following the announcement from Starbucks, Grande—who has a love of clouds, even selling a Cloud perfume (Cloud Eau de Parfum)—tweeted celebrating the release of the Cloud Macchiato. Grande, rocking a Starbucks barista apron, was seen at home with her dogs, drinking a Cloud Macchiato and accompanied by two baristas.

Ariana Grande is a well-known vegan and has spoken freely and given many interviews on the benefits of a plant-based diet. Arianators, as fans of the pop star are called, were shocked and disappointed that the star would promote a drink that clearly is not a vegan option. While the milk may be substituted for soy, the cloud foam definitely contains egg whites, of which there is no substitute. Peiper continued the description, "To create the Cloud Macchiato, Starbucks' in-house product development team created a special recipe for cloud powder, using egg whites as a key ingredient to create a layer of fluffy cloud foam."

While the Cloud Macchiato is still associated with Ariana Grande—some people ask the baristas for the Ariana Grande drink—the fervor continues. Confusion and controversy has been stirred, as many vegans simply assume since Ariana Grande promoted the drink, it is naturally vegan. Online posts indicate Arianators are disappointed in Grande as she did not stick to her convictions, and baristas are tired of explaining that the Cloud Macchiato is not vegan. Still others admit perhaps Grande did not even know the ingredients that went into making this tasty treat. Perhaps the public will never know.

Starbucks Annual Holiday Cups

Since 1997, Starbucks has designed a unique holiday cup—a celebration and nod to the upcoming Christmas season. A perusal through past designs suggest festive holiday themes including Christmas trees, ornaments, ice skates, wrapping paper, mittens, snowflakes, carolers, and reindeers. Except for the first two years—in 1997 the cup was released in four jeweled tones and in 1998 the cup was purple—the cup has taken on various shades of red. That is why you hear people refer to the Starbucks holiday design as the red cup. For nearly two decades, the holiday cups were highly anticipated by Starbucks loyalists and enjoyed by many.

The holiday cup took a controversial turn in 2015, and with the explosion on social media, the cup unveiling has become an annual annoyance to some. A Starbucks Stories release, dated November 9, 2015 ("The Story Behind the Design of Starbucks Red Holiday Cups"), described the cup as a "two-toned ombré design, with a bright poppy color on top that shades into a darker cranberry below." Starbucks had taken a minimalist approach with a no-design cup, which would allow customers to doodle holiday designs and "create their own stories with a red cup that mimics a blank canvas." Starbucks devotees know it is common practice to draw on the annual cups, so that year the company was providing an empty cup canvas for their art.

The eruption that stirred across the globe started with a former pastor and social media evangelist, Joshua Feuerstein. Outside a Starbucks, holiday cup in hand, Feuerstein posted a video to his Facebook page, proclaiming, "Do you realize that Starbucks wanted to take Christ and Christmas off of the brand-new cups? That's why they are just plain red." The social media furry ensued, insisting with the minimalist theme missing trees and trimmings, that Starbucks wanted to eliminate Christmas. It was a war on Christmas. Postings, social media, news anchors, and late-night comics all seemed to weigh in on the red cup; even hardcore Starbucks customers suggested the plain red cup lacked Christmas spirit.

On November 1, 2016, a new green unity cup was introduced in U.S. Starbucks stores, a week ahead of the presidential election. The green cup featured a mosaic of many people drawn in one continuous line, designed to signify the connections customers and partners share as a community. Online media was ablaze with many mistaking the green cup for their holiday-themed cup; even some news media outlets falsely reported the information. Even after the mix-up became apparent, some found the green cups too political and were not fans. Starbucks was prepared to eliminate any controversy with the holiday cup that year, inviting customers to share their cup designs in a holiday cup competition. With over 1,200 customer submissions, ultimately thirteen cups were chosen to be produced, representing the spirit of the holidays around the world. Released on November 10 were twelve red holiday cups featuring designs such as holiday lights, candy canes, ornaments, a poinsettia plant, and an evergreen forest, plus one cold beverage cup with a wooden wreath encircling the Starbucks logo.

In 2017, Starbucks released a very different holiday cup. What was the immediate shock? The cup was not red, but white, with red highlights plus a splash of green. The cup was specifically designed to be a coloring opportunity for customers to add color and their own illustration. The bottom of the cup showed a pair of hands holding red cups of coffee, which were connected with swirling ribbons. Also featured on the cup was holiday décor such as wrapping paper, snowflakes, doves, and a Christmas tree. At the top there are two interlocked hands, representing two individuals holding hands. The controversy this year was over the hand holding, some interpreting the two hands represented a same-sex couple and that Starbucks was promoting a gay agenda. Jordan Kay from Starbucks Creative Studio, illustrator of the holiday cup, noted in a November 1, 2017, news release ("Starbucks Holiday Cup Comes with a Message to 'Give Good'"), "I liked the idea of hands as the centering point, a symbol of connection, love and giving joy." She continued, "Whether it's wrapping presents or decorating a tree, writing cards or enjoying a mug of cocoa." Kay's intent was to promote kindness.

In 2018, possibly in an attempt to avoid the controversies of years past, on November 1 the company released four holiday cups just like they did in 1997, but this time all highly festive. The four included a red holiday cup featuring bands of bright red poppy and a darker cranberry, a white cup with mint leaves and ripe coffee cherries, a red and white houndstooth design, and a design of stars set in interlocking diamonds in various shades of Starbucks green. The more festive designs appeared to satisfy customers, and social media was receptive to the unveiling. The controversy came with a new reusable cup. The next day Starbucks released its red reusable cup. If you ordered a holiday drink on this day, you were to receive a free red reusable cup. This was a reusable cup that came with a discount on future drinks; any customer who came back after 2:00 p.m. and used the cup could get 50 cents off their Grande drink order during the holiday season. Supplies of the cup were limited, and many stores ran out of the free cups within hours after opening. The date had been promoted by Starbucks, anticipated by many, and caused many individuals to leave the coffeehouse disappointed and irritated. We all know what it is like to wait in line for some time and then be told the item you are looking for is no longer available. Needless to say, many people took to social media to share their dissatisfaction.

The holiday cups released on November 7 for 2019 met with minimal criticism. Four designs were released in holiday red and green colors. The well-received selections included Polka Dots (a red cup with green dots and mini sirens), Candy Cane Stripes (bold red and white stripes on the cup with a green siren, and STARBUCKS lettering), Merry Dance (red and green "Merry Coffee" on a white cup), and Merry Stripes (a green cup with "Merry Coffee" wording on the stripes). Can you guess the criticism? If you said, "Starbucks doesn't want to say Merry Christmas so they decided to wish Merry Coffee," you would be correct.

On November 6, 2020, the holiday cups were released for the season. Instead of debate the 2020 cups were largely met with harmony and accolades; released in the midst of the COVID-19 pandemic, many wondered if the company would continue the tradition. In a year of social isolation and depression for many, the tradition of releasing the holiday cups was a welcome distraction to lighten one's spirit, with the theme "Carry the Merry." The Creative Director for Starbucks, Jeff Wilkson shared, "Our thought behind the cups this year was about people carrying them out in the world as messages of joy" (a Starbucks Stories release, dated November 5, 2020, "The Holiday Season Has Arrived at Starbucks"). The options included Ribbon (a cup of ribbons of brand greens and red), Dot (red and green polka dots adorn this cup with a ribbon "carry the merry"), Sparkle (a red cup with glittering holiday ornaments), and Brand Wrap (a modern version of a ribbon design on this cup featuring the Starbucks wordmark).

What will next year bring to the holiday cup roundtable discussion? One can only speculate, but the cup controversy will likely continue.

Starbucks Copes with Tragedy

Starbucks has had its share of sadness through the years. Notably, late on July 6, 1997, after a long Fourth of July weekend, tragedy struck at a Georgetown Starbucks coffee shop in Washington, D.C. Early on that Monday morning, at 5:15 a.m., the dayshift manager arrived to find three Starbucks employees shot to death in an apparent botched theft. Nothing had been stolen, and no fingerprints were left at the scene. A bullet hole was found over the safe, but the safe had not been opened. Starbucks offered a $100,000 reward for information leading to the arrest and conviction of the person or people responsible for the crime, and $10,000 was put up by the Georgetown Business Association. Forensic psychologist and Tru TV's Crime Library contributor Katherine Ramsland wrote about the case on www.trutv.com:

> Starbucks decided to reopen the shop, announcing a reopening date of February 21, 1998. To honor the victims, they built a floor-to-ceiling Maplewood mural that held three boxes, each engraved with the initials of

one of the victims. Their surviving relatives placed mementos into the boxes, and the company announced it would donate all net profits from this store to the Community Foundation for the National Capital Region, an organization dedicated to nonviolence. Starbucks also gave money to Circle of Hope, a group that guided teens toward being productive members of society.

In June 1998, after an *America's Most Wanted* segment on the shootings had aired on TV for a second time, a tip came in that pointed to Carl Derek Cooper. Cooper, a DC-area man in his late twenties, was arrested and brought to justice. Finally, on April 25, 2000, he avoided a possible death sentence by pleading guilty to a multitude of crimes, including the three Starbucks employee murders. The judge sentenced him to life in prison with no chance of parole.

A decade later, tragedy struck again at a Starbucks store in St. Louis, Missouri. Good Samaritan Roger Kreutz, 54 years old, was struck by a car while trying to prevent a crime. He died from his injuries two days later. Kreutz was a regular at his local Starbucks coffee shop and witnessed two thieves stealing the tip jar money. He ran outside Starbucks chasing them and was run over by the getaway car. The thieves left the scene but were later apprehended. There was only around $5 in the tip jar.

Maneuvering the Coronavirus Pandemic

An outbreak of a highly contagious coronavirus, otherwise referred to as COVID-19, started in Wuhan, China, in December 2019 and quickly spread around the globe. According to the World Health Organization, the coronavirus, which brings respiratory issues ranging from mild to lethal, had spread globally to every continent, with 223 countries and territories reporting. In early 2021, the virus had already peaked and leveled off in China, the country of origin, with the United States reporting over 550,000 deaths. (For a daily update of the number of COVID-19 cases and deaths, by country, consult the World Health Organization's Coronavirus Dashboard at https://www.who.int.)

At the start of March 2020, COVID-19 was making its way across the United States, touching Starbucks personally on March 6. The ill employee worked at a downtown Seattle Starbucks Reserve bar. While this location was temporarily closed and underwent a strict cleaning regime, the employee was sent home to quarantine and recover. Emergency measures quickly hastened to address the numerous other cases that followed. The company had already implemented a pandemic routine after half of its stores closed in China and immediately activated procedures to sanitize and thwart the spread of the coronavirus. By the end of March 2020 roughly 95 percent of Starbucks stores in China were open, initially with limited lobby hours and minimal seating. The company found a successful strategy with the pandemic in China, which was helpful in other locations, both domestic and international. The months that followed were a time of quick response by Starbucks in order to protect the health of both partners and customers. Adaptations to regular routines included pausing the use of reusable cups, offering drive-thru service only, contactless delivery, limited hours, and store closures.

Since Starbucks is known for its social gathering and Third Place culture, this disease has caused some baristas to be fearful of coming to work. Why? The coronavirus is spread through close person-to-person contact—respiratory droplets from someone who is infected. Droplets can easily travel from someone sneezing, coughing, or even talking in close proximity. Although in mid-March Starbucks eventually closed all U.S. stores to in-store traffic, changing to drive-thru or delivery service only, many baristas expressed health worries as the coronavirus spread feverishly. Following voiced concerns, Starbucks stepped up to protect the health and welfare of retail partners with catastrophe and enhanced pay programs. The Starbucks Foundation additionally invested over $9 million in response to COVID-19 in order to support a variety of community programs. At the end of fiscal 2020, nearly all of the Starbucks company-operated and licensed stores were reopened.

In early 2021, Starbucks became part of a group effort to support Washington state and Governor Jay Inslee in a task of improving vaccination distribution in the state. Inslee has formed a Washington State Vaccine Command and Coordination Center, a public and private partnership with a goal of delivering more vaccinees. Starbucks is joined by Microsoft, Costco, Kaiser Permanente, and other organizations. The Starbucks group is working on developing the following models: vaccination clinics, drive-through clinics, and mobile pop-ups to serve those in rural or underserved areas. In a press release from the company ("Offering to Serve: Starbucks Joins Effort to Help Speed COVID-19 Vaccination Delivery," January 19, 2021) the aim is clear, "Starbucks is focused on assisting with operational efficiency, developing models for vaccination centers that can be standardized and reproduced across the state and helping improve the patient experience."

Coffee Controversy Timeline

2004: The first Starbucks employee union is formed.

2005: Starbucks purchases Ethos Water for $7.7 million.

2010: The CERT sues Starbucks and other coffee companies to reduce the amount of acrylamide in coffee.

2012: Bad publicity in the United Kingdom centered around Starbucks' tax avoidance.

2014: Barista Kristie Williams started a petition on Coworker.org for Starbucks employees to be allowed to display their tattoos.

2015: Starbucks holiday cup angers many for not being festive enough or symbolizing Christmas.

2015: Ethos Water bottling operation is moved from drought-stricken California to Pennsylvania.

2016: Barista Jaime Prater started a petition on Cowroker.org noting the lack of labor is killing morale.

2018: Los Angeles judge rules that coffee sold in California must have a cancer warning.

2018: Starbucks announces plastic straws will be replaced with new strawless lids globally by 2020.

2018: Starbucks announces the closing of 150 underperforming stores in fiscal year 2019.

2018: Two African American men arrested in a Philadelphia Starbucks for chatting and not making a purchase.

2019: Vegan Ariana Grande helps Starbucks launch Cloud Macchiato, a drink made with egg whites.

2019: California rules that no cancer warning label will be required on coffee.

2020: Starbucks takes safety and health actions in order to protect partners and customers from COVID-19.

2021: In an effort to fight COVID-19 and increase vaccinations, Starbucks joins Washington State Vaccine Command and Coordination Center.

CHAPTER TEN

Starbucks and Schultz: Planning for the Future

Success should not be measured in dollars: It's about how you conduct the journey, and how big your heart is at the end of it.
—Howard Schultz, Chairman Emeritus Starbucks,
Pour Your Heart into It (1997)

Company Stock

Starbucks stock is traded on the National Association of Securities Dealers Automated Quotations (NASDAQ) under the symbol SBUX. To learn more about the NASDAQ exchange, its operations, and investment opportunities, check out the website at https://www.nasdaq.com. Starbucks Corporation went public on June 26, 1992, at a price of $17 per share (this equates to $0.27 per share, adjusted for six subsequent stock splits). It closed on the first day of trading at $21.50 (or $0.34 per share, on a split-adjusted basis).

The company's stock has had significant momentum over the past year. This is excellent news for the approximately 18,000 shareholders of record, according to a recently filed SEC report. Hovering just over $100, the stock has more than doubled with a fifty-two-week high of $107.75 and a low of $50.02. The positive uptick in the stock's price builds from a number of factors, including favorable financial results for the company, digital engagement, the success and growth opportunities found in the Chinese market, and adaptation during the COVID-19 pandemic.

Starbucks Financial Snapshot

Snapshots and overviews of a stock are all similar in content and pack a powerful punch of information. Starbucks is listed on NASDAQ's Global Select (GS) Market, the most selective tier of companies meeting the highest financial requirements. Check out the trading symbol SBUX on any of the online financial sites and you can see up-to-date trading quote activity. You can also get such information as historical prices, stock charts, company news and information, recent headlines, and financials.

A great deal of information can be gleaned from a quick overview. Price data, market swings, and earnings and dividend statistics are essential to explore when considering the buying or selling of a stock. Table 10.1 shows an example of a snapshot quote after trading on Friday, January 22, 2021.

The stock closed on January 22, 2021 at 4 p.m. ET at $103.91; that was the final price of the day. If you wanted to buy a share of Starbucks stock, you would have had to pay $103.91 at that time. This was $0.67 lower than the previous close of $104.58 on January 21, 2021. Volume shows how many shares of SBUX were traded on a particular day, and in this case, there were 5,230,400 shares of Starbucks stock traded on January 22, 2021. The trading volume information is important to watch because a wide swing away from a typical trading day means there is some kind of news—either good or bad—that has caused investors to

Table 10.1 Starbucks Corporation (SBUX: NASDAQ Exchange)

CLOSE $103.91 **January 22, 2021**
Previous Close $104.58
Open $104.16
Day's range $103.06–$104.47
52-week range $50.02–$107.75
Avg. volume (10 days) 5.2 M
Market cap 122.0 B
Shares outstanding 1.17 B
PE ratio (TTM) 131.53
EPS (TTM) 0.79
Dividend $1.80
Ex-dividend date 02/17/21
Dividend pay date 03/05/21

increase trading in Starbucks stock. This is pertinent information if you are an investor and a red flag about possible company-impacting news for anyone interested in Starbucks.

While the stock closed at $104.58 on January 21, after-hours trading resulted in the stock opening up the next trading day down at $104.16 per share. SBUX reached a high during the day of January 22 at $104.47 (the best price if you were selling the stock) and a low of $103.06 (the deal of the day if you were buying the stock). *Tip*: In the stock market, you always want to buy low and sell high.

The fifty-two-week range tells the low and high of the stock's price fluctuations over a one-year period. It was a bumpy year for 2020, with prices cut in half, in the low $50 range, during the COVID-19 stock market crash in March and progressively rising back to the near $100 level. What has caused the exceptional growth? Many factors, including the ability to adapt to the COVID-19 business model coupled with the fact that analysts are hot on Starbucks—their future revenue, earnings, and growth opportunities. Keep in mind that when analysts make positive recommendations and increase ratings, stocks typically rise. Nevertheless, a wise investor will listen to the comments from analysts but also independently read, study, and analyze information and data before making investment decisions.

Market Cap stands for market capitalization and shows the total value of the company on a given day—here, roughly $122 billion. Investors look at the number as an indicator of company size. You arrive at that figure by multiplying the stock price times the total number of shares outstanding. This number gives the total, theoretically, of what it would cost to buy the entire company. Here's a rough calculation: $104 × 1.17 billion shares = $122 billion.

Volume shows that on average over the previous ten days, there were 5.2 million shares traded daily. Again, this is good to know as a base for trading. A high number relative to the average volume may suggest a macro event in the economy. It might be a major gross domestic product (GDP) announcement, which is a benchmark output indicator for the entire U.S. economy; or it could be something happening within the company, such as a switch in the executive officers or a shift in financials or a global event like the COVID-19 pandemic. That actually happened on Monday, March 16, 2020, often referred to as Black Monday; many may deem this the height and uncertainty of the pandemic scare. The Dow hit a new record, losing 2,997.10, which equates to a 12.93 percent drop. That scare and uncertainty generated a lot of buying and selling in Starbucks stock, with 23,345,900 shares traded that day.

The earnings per share (EPS) figure is Starbucks' net income over the trailing, or preceding, twelve months (TTM), divided by its number of shares outstanding. The simple EPS calculation uses only actual outstanding shares of a company's stock. EPS can provide investors with an idea of a company's profitability and is one factor in how much investors would be willing to pay for the stock. EPS TTM is $0.79, representing the portion of the company's profit allocated to each common stock share, fallen from the previous year at $2.92 primarily due to the impact of COVID-19 closings and limited service. Earnings are reported by a company on a quarterly basis, four times a year. The EPS is a widely used measure of value of a company and highly monitored by investors and analysts. Analysts prepare EPS projections and when a stock beats or falls short of projections, stock prices can move greatly. Watch for an announcement called "Earnings Call," the quarterly conference call when the management of the company discusses earnings and financial results with investors and analysts.

The P/E is the price-to-earnings Ratio. The P/E is calculated by taking the price of the stock and dividing it by the earnings per share of the stock. The earnings are usually taken from the TTM. The P/E tells, theoretically, how much an investor is willing to pay for $1 of a company's earnings. A P/E of 131.53 means that Starbucks has $1 in annual per-share earnings for every $131.53 in share price. P/E is often misinterpreted by the investment community and should really be viewed only in terms of long-term trends. But, generally speaking, companies that are expected to grow and have higher earnings in the future should have a higher P/E than those that are in a downward trend. At a 131.53 P/E, the stock has a fairly high stock price compared to earnings, indicating there may be high expectations for future earnings.

Dividends are the part of the net earnings of a company that are distributed to shareholders. Starbucks pays a dividend at the current quarterly rate of $0.45 per share or $1.80 a year. Quite simply, for every share of stock one owns you will receive a total yearly dividend of $1.80. High dividend paying stocks, which also have the potential for capital appreciation, are a win–win. Note the *Ex-div. date*, which means without a dividend. If you buy a stock that pays a dividend, this date is important. In this case, if you buy Starbucks on or after the ex-dividend date, of February 17, 2021, you aren't entitled to the next dividend. Conversely, if you buy the stock before the ex-dividend date, you receive the dividend payment on March 5, 2021.

To keep up with Starbucks stock and to monitor the company's financial performance, see the Investor Relations page on their corporate website.

Did You Know?

According to the National Coffee Association, American coffee drinkers consume about three cups of coffee each day, on average.

Commodity Price Risk

Risk exists in every company. Executives monitor business risk in order to manage future uncertainties and still achieve strong performance. Banks must prepare for a sudden shift in interest rates, school systems for shifting demographics, and contractors for an increase in raw material prices. The primary market risk for Starbucks? Commodity price risk.

Starbucks uses two major commodities—coffee and dairy. The price and availability of these commodities can impact operations and the bottom line. The company sells whole-bean and ground coffee, along with utilizing coffee in a number of prepared drinks. So, when the price of coffee goes up, it can be a problem for coffee companies like Starbucks. Starbucks also pays a premium for the high-quality arabica coffee it utilizes. The company is fairly successful, however, at locking into contracts and hedging its risks. According to the 10-K for fiscal 2018, the company has good relations with suppliers—coffee producers, outside trading companies, and exporters—so the risk of nondelivery on commitments is small. The good news for Starbucks and its shareholders is that the company's recent 10-K report for the thirteen weeks ending June 30, 2019, reported that there had been no material change in the commodity price risk.

The company also purchases significant amounts of dairy products, particularly fluid milk, to support its retail stores' needs. While noting an increase in the cost of milk due to shortages, delays, or interruptions in processing—particularly in the international market—could adversely affect the company's profit, the company maintains that risk of milk not being delivered is remote. Starbucks has worked to maintain strong relationships with its dairy suppliers. The company has also moved from whole milk to low-fat 2 percent milk as standard. It's not only healthier but is also less expensive—a positive health move and also a good cost-cutting move.

Did You Know?

Coffee was introduced in North America circa 1668, but it didn't become popular as an American drink until after the famous Boston Tea Party of 1773. On December 16, 1773, a group of colonists, disguised as American Indians, boarded three British ships and dumped 342 crates of tea into Boston Harbor. That was a lot of tea—45 tons of it. It was a direct act of protest by American colonists who were angry at the British government. Three years before, in 1770, colonial opposition and boycotting of imported British goods had caused the British Parliament to withdraw all of the Townshend Act's taxes, except one; it retained the heavy tax on imported British tea.

The situation remained relatively quiet as American colonists simply evaded the tax by smuggling tea into the colonies from Holland. But this was not good for the British East India Company, which had been left holding huge surpluses of tea and was financially faltering. The British government wanted to save the tea company from bankruptcy. So, in May 1773, Parliament gave the company a refund, or *drawback*, of the entire shilling-per-pound duty, which allowed the company to sell tea more cheaply than the Dutch smugglers. It was assumed that Americans would buy the cheaper tea, despite the tax, rather than the higher-priced smuggled tea from Holland. This would uphold the principle of parliamentary taxation and also save the tea company from ruin. American colonists condemned the act. They saw it as taxation without representation, and many people boycotted buying and drinking tea as a protest. Although the movement away from drinking tea was short-lived, coffee became a fashionable drink and a substitute for tea.

The Future of the Company

In order for a business to be successful, the leaders must be forward thinking. Executives must have a detailed execution plan with metric targets, innovative ideas, and financial goals in place. Often referred to as a growth strategy, it is a targeted plan for long-term success.

The future of Starbucks is being tended by CEO and President Kevin Johnson, an exceptional executive staff, and the board of directors. Starbucks had developed growth strategies, even revealing a detailed growth strategy at the 2018 Annual meeting. The numbers and detailed strategies are best left to the company leaders, but it is clear the future of the company lies in the following key areas.

Expand Business Partnerships

Starbucks has developed a wide variety of business partnerships—Spotify, Uber Eats, Nestlé, and a multitude of licensees are just a few examples of business partnerships with similar-minded companies that will grow

Starbucks. These partnerships take advantage of particular niches and supply chains that benefit both parties. Starbucks customers can access music on Spotify while the media company gets a new group of devotees. Uber Eats is the prime delivery method for Starbucks and this means big bucks for the online food ordering platform, while Starbucks increases sales by meeting the delivery needs of its customers. The Starbucks and Nestlé partnership gives Nestlé the opportunity to add Starbucks to its single-serve capsule systems and provides Starbucks access to Nestlé's 190-country distribution channel. Watch for more action on the partnership front, like the recently developed partnership with Alibaba for coffee delivery in China.

Digital Innovation

The company will continue to be at the forefront of technology in the coffee industry. Look for detailed seed-to-cup traceability and enhanced mobile order and pay features. Digital personalization and customization will be enhanced to attract more customers on a global scale. Drive-thru opportunities will be increased in order to accommodate the fast-paced lifestyle of coffee lovers. Virtual Starbucks stores, like the one recently launched in China in partnership with Alibaba, may become more plentiful as a method to enhance digital involvement. Customers can use an app to easily order coffee or merchandise, have it delivered, or even send a Starbucks digital gift card to someone.

New Imaginations in Food and Beverage

The Reserve Roasteries and Reserve Coffee concept will continue to grow, catering to ultra-sophisticated coffee consumers. The Teavana tea line, purchased by Starbucks in 2013, will be a winner as the company expands offerings in this line. Asian countries are big tea drinkers and as stores spread globally, new Teavana products are sure to be introduced. More drinks like Nitro Cold Brew, the company's newest standout, will be coming from the Tryer Lab. And finally, as health, nutrition, and wellness remain on the minds of consumers around the world, Starbucks will continue to provide healthy drink and food choices for customers. Look for not only new products, but continued updating of the caloric and nutritional breakdown of the items on their menus.

Markets

Much of the new growth for Starbucks will come from outside the United States in untapped international markets. The company has been quite vocal—international expansion, particularly in the China market segment, is a key driver for the future. The Q3 2019 Earnings Call reported, "Our total store count in China grew by 16% vs. prior year to more than 3,900 stores at the end of Q3 2019." International growth is essential to maintain the company's profitability and Starbucks executives know of its importance. John Culver serves as group president, International, Channel Development and Global Coffee & Tea, and is keen on long-term viability in the country. At the Q1 2019 Earnings Conference Call, Culver explained, "And I would just say that we continue to take the long-term view and belief in our strategy in executing in a way that continues to elevate the experience for our customers. As a company in China, we're not looking to buy short-term revenue. Rather, we're looking at continuing to build on the 20-year history and the success that we've had in the market."

China is the future, but Starbucks likely has some surprises in store for additional new markets. In June 2019, the company's eightieth global market was reached when the first store in Malta, on the Valletta Waterfront, was opened. "Whether it's China, Japan, or our licensed markets, these are the very early days of our growth across our International business," stressed Culver at the 2020 Investor Day. Clearly, Culver and his team have plans for an international reach.

It is not just about retail store expansion. In 2012, Starbucks opened its sixth roasting plant in Augusta, Georgia. Originally it produced soluble products and recently added whole-bean roasters. The plant joined four other U.S. roasting plants which are located in Kent, Washington; York, Pennsylvania; Carson Valley, Nevada; and Sandy Run, South Carolina. It was in 2003 that Starbucks opened its only roasting plant outside the United States in Amsterdam, The Netherlands. The Amsterdam roasting plant is a 97,000-square-foot facility, ideally located for shipping and distributing freshly roasted product to Europe. When the next Starbucks roasting facility is planned, it's likely the international market will be a contender.

Social Mission

Starbucks is not just about coffee. The business is also about human connections and people. The company is a stock-owned firm, yet it continues to balance profitability with a social conscience and agenda, and their customers approve. Working to make coffee the world's first sustainable agricultural product, ethically sourcing coffee, reducing its environmental impact, and contributing to strengthening communities, Starbucks is making a global social impact. Whether it be with the Starbucks Foundation, supporting youth and origin communities, welcoming refugees, hiring veterans and military spouses, embracing green, investing in its coffee communities, or promoting pay equity—to name just a few—the company is widely known as being socially responsible.

Chairman Emeritus Schultz

In June 2018, Howard Schultz retired from Starbucks, yet many still and will always associate him with the company. Rightfully so, as it was Schultz's vision and tenacity that shifted Starbucks from a small regional coffeehouse into massive global fame. Schultz has demonstrated the ability to think on a macro level. It was no surprise that in January 2019 this exceptionally skilled business executive announced he would consider running for the 2020 U.S. Presidential election as a "centrist independent." Unfortunately, back surgery in the summer of 2019 caused Schultz to pull up camp on his presidential bid work and in September 2019 he made a public statement that he no longer would consider a run for the top political seat.

Many Starbucks devotees would no doubt have enjoyed a Schultz for Presidency campaign. Many of the skills Schultz developed and sharpened while leading Starbucks could have been exemplified on the presidential level. Managing the finances of a global corporate powerhouse would be great practice to assist in managing the $4.8 trillion plus U.S. budget. Schultz spurred global expansion for Starbucks, and the skills utilized in understanding different cultures and temperaments could assist in international negotiations for the country. Dealing with people on a daily basis and Schultz's selling skills would have been an asset in high-powered domestic and international negotiations.

So, what is the former Starbucks executive doing in his retirement? Schultz, living in Seattle, has plenty of opportunities to utilize his exceptional skills and still have influence on people and policy. He was given the title of Chairman Emeritus by the Starbucks board, a lifetime honor. He and his wife Sheri co-lead the Schultz Family Foundation, focusing on needs like Opportunity Youth and Post-9/11 Veterans. Schultz has written three books: *Pour Your Heart into It* (1997), *Onward: How Starbucks Fought for Its Life without Losing Its Soul* (2011), and most recently, *From the Ground Up* (2019). The books include stories of his personal and company journeys and life lessons from his rich and fulfilled life. His legacy is entrenched at Starbucks, for it is after all and always will be the "Third Place."

The Outlook

Starbucks built its success on using high-quality arabica coffee beans in lieu of commercially mass-produced coffee. And Starbucks is not willing to give up its promise of exceptional taste in its fine coffees, teas, specialty drinks, and food products. It may be considered a small luxury, but loyal Starbucks customers have not been deterred. It continues to be the number one gourmet specialty coffee retailer in the world.

Where will Starbucks be in the next decade—2030? The exceptional foundation set by Howard Schultz and successors like Kevin Johnson will bring innovative products and experiences for the coffee powerhouse. People will still be drinking coffee. Coffee is, after all, the second most consumed beverage after water. New markets are emerging, but the Chinese market will be vast—likely larger than the U.S. market—as their economy is expected to outpace the United States in the next decade. At Investor Day held on December 9, 2020, it was announced that the company believes they will reach 55,000 stores in hundred markets by 2030.

As Starbucks looks ahead, one keystone it can build on is its well-known concern about the communities that support its stores and the broader world community. Ultimately, this will be the mainstay for the company's future survival. In good economic times, or when bad times hit, Starbucks makes it a mission to be a socially conscious company through which customers can get involved in helping some great causes. Drink a cup of coffee, it says, and make the world a better place. Starbucks makes it clear: It is a down-to-earth company and is here for the long run.

Timeline

1971   The first Starbucks store opens in the trendy Seattle Pike Place Market.

1972   Second Starbucks Coffee store opens in Seattle.

1982   Howard Schultz joins the company as director of retail operations and marketing.

1983   Schultz travels to Italy for Starbucks to attend an international house-wares show in Milan. He is impressed with the espresso bars he visits there and sees the potential to develop a similar Italian-style coffee culture for Starbucks.

1984   Schultz finally persuades the founders to allow him to put the coffee-house concept to a test in their downtown Seattle store, where the espresso bar concept is embraced by customers.

1985   Schultz leaves to start up his own company Il Giornale, an Italian-style coffeehouse. Il Giornale offers brewed coffee and espresso beverages made from Starbucks coffee beans.

1987   Il Giornale acquires the Starbucks assets and changes the name to Starbucks Corporation.

       Howard Schultz returns to Starbucks as president and CEO.

       The first Starbucks stores outside of Seattle are opened, in Chicago and Vancouver, BC.

1988   Starbucks offers part-time employees (working 20 or more hours) the same health coverage as full-timers.

1991   Starbucks becomes the first private company to offer a company-wide stock option plan that includes part-time workers.

       The first licensed airport Starbucks store is opened.

1992   Starbucks goes public with an IPO, becoming the first specialty coffee company to go public.

1993   Opens a second roasting facility in Kent, WA.

1995   Starbucks starts selling compact disc (CD) music compilations.

The company begins serving Frappuccino blended beverages.

The company opens a third roasting plant in York, PA.

1996   Starbucks International introduces its first stores outside of North America, in Tokyo and Singapore.

1997   CEO Howard Schultz donates the proceeds from his book, *Pour Your Heart into It*, in order to establish the Starbucks Foundation.

1998   The company launches Starbucks.com.

Starbucks announces plans to sell coffee in supermarkets nationwide through an agreement with Kraft.

1999   Starbucks begins a partnership with Conservation International to promote methods of coffee growing that are environmentally responsible.

2000   Orin Smith is promoted to president and CEO of the company.

Howard Schultz transitions from chairman and CEO to chairman and chief global strategist.

2001   Starbucks begins to offer high-speed wireless internet access in select stores.

The Starbucks Card is unveiled—a prepaid purchasing card customers can use and reload.

The company developed socially responsible coffee buying guidelines called C.A.F.E. Practices (Coffee and Farmer Equity Practices).

2002   The company publishes its first Corporate Social Responsibility (CSR) report.

2003   Starbucks acquires Seattle Coffee Company.

The company opens new roasting facilities in Carson Valley, NV, and overseas in Amsterdam, The Netherlands.

2004   The company opened its first Farmer Support Center in San José, Costa Rica.

The first Starbucks Union is formed.

The Starbucks Coffee Master program is introduced for partners to gain more expertise about the world of coffee.

2005   Orin Smith retires as Starbucks president and CEO.

Jim Donald is promoted to president and CEO.

Starbucks purchases Ethos Water.

2006   Distribution agreement is signed with the North American Coffee Partnership to distribute Ethos Water.

Starbucks becomes the first company in the United States to use 10 percent PCF in their hot beverage cups.

Starbucks Farmer Support Center opened in Guatemala City.

2007   Converts to 2 percent milk as a beverage standard in the United States and Canada.

2008   Jim Donald is out as head of the company.

Howard Schultz returns as CEO to mend the financially troubled coffeehouse.

Starbucks announces it will close approximately 600 U.S. stores to improve long-term profitable growth.

Starbucks tests $1 (8 oz.) short brew in Seattle.

Starbucks launches its first online suggestion website at www.mystarbucksidea.com, an online community for customer input of ideas.

2009   Starbucks opens its fifth roasting plant in Sandy Run, SC.

The company launches My Starbucks Rewards loyalty program.

A company announcement is made increasing the company's fiscal 2009 cost reduction target from $400 million to $500 million. Efforts include closing 300 more stores and reducing employees by 6,700.

Free unlimited Wi-Fi offered in stores.

Starbucks Farmer Support Center opened in Kigali, Rwanda.

2010   The Council of Education and Research on Toxics (CERT) sues Starbucks, along with over ninety other coffee companies.

2011   The company debuts a streamlined logo, eliminating the words Starbucks Coffee and removing the circle around the siren.

Starbucks Farmer Support Center opened in Mbeya, Tanzania.

2012   Lightest Starbucks Roast, Blonde Roast, is introduced.

Starbucks Farmer Support Centers opened in Manizales, Colombia, and Yunnan, China.

2013   Costa Rica coffee farm, Hacienda Alsacia, is purchased.

2014   The company opens its first Reserve Roastery in Seattle.

The Starbucks College Achievement Plan is launched through Arizona State University.

Starbucks Farmer Support Center opened in Addis Ababa, Ethiopia.

2015   The company reaches 99 percent ethically sourced coffee.

Kevin Johnson is appointed president and COO.

The company launched its One Tree for Every Bag commitment.

Starbucks Farmer Support Center opened in North Sumatra, Indonesia.

2016   Music service, Spotify, is added in retail stores.

The original Costa Rica Farmer Support Center is relocated from San José to the Hacienda Alsacia.

Starbucks Farmer Support Center opened in Chiapas, Mexico.

Starbucks becomes a founding member of the Sustainable Coffee Challenge.

2017   Shanghai Roastery opens.

Kevin Johnson becomes CEO.

Howard Schultz transitions to executive chairman.

Starbucks Global Academy is launched as an online tool to strengthen careers and community.

2018   Howard Schultz retires from Starbucks, leaving with the title Chairman Emeritus.

Plastic straws are out, being replaced by a strawless lid by 2020.

Virtual store in China opens in partnership with Alibaba.

Milan Roastery opens.

New York Roastery opens.

Tryer Lab opens at Seattle Headquarters.

Starbucks and Nestlé form a Global Business Alliance.

Partnering with Uber Eats, Starbucks Delivers is launched.

2019   Seattle store becomes cashless.

Tokyo Roastery opens, followed by the Chicago Roastery later in the year.

Starbucks ranked #5 on *Fortune's 2019* The World's Most Admired Companies.

Cloud Macchiato launched with assistance from Ariana Grande.

The company reports consolidated net revenues of $26.5 billion for the fiscal year.

2020   Goal of training 200,000 farmers by year end, 160,000 farmers trained by farming and agronomy center at mid-year.

Health and well-being of customers and employees force strategic decisions to navigate COVID-19, such as safety protocols, closing stores, reducing store hours, and serving drive-thru only.

The in-person March 18 shareholder annual meeting is rescheduled from the WaMu Theater to a virtual webcast format due to COVID-19 health concerns.

Business downturn due to COVID-19, but company deems situation is temporary.

Fiscal 2020 closes the year with 32,660 stores in eighty-three countries.

The company announced the goal of 55,000 stores in hundred markets by 2030.

2021 The March 17 shareholder annual meeting is scheduled as a virtual webcast, rather than in person, due to COVID-19 health concerns.

Sources: Personal research including data obtained from press releases and Company Timeline, available at https://www.starbucks.com.

Glossary

Acidity The quality that makes coffee sharp and refreshing. A tangy taste experienced mainly on the edges of your tongue and at the back of the palate. Coffee needs a level of acidity; otherwise, it will taste flat. As the roast develops, the coffee acidity falls.

Aftertaste The sensation of coffee vapors that remains in your mouth after swallowing.

Americano A style of coffee made by combining hot water with espresso. The strength of an Americano can vary depending on the amount of water and the amount of espresso added. The strength can be increased by increasing the number of shots of espresso.

Arabica The earliest cultivated coffee and the most widely grown. It is considered to produce the highest quality of coffee (see *robusta*). This species is grown at higher altitudes and prefers to be grown in shade. The taste is more refined, milder, aromatic, and flavorful. It can be dark roasted for a bold taste.

Aroma A distinctive, pleasant odor. Aroma involves the art of smelling coffee and is difficult to separate from flavor. It gives you the first hint of how your coffee will taste.

Bag A burlap sack of coffee used to ship the commodity around the globe. Weight may differ by country, but the most common measurement of a bag is 60 kilograms or 132 pounds.

Balance A coffee quality in which no single characteristic of the coffee overwhelms the others.

Barista A person professionally trained in the art of making espresso. This term is often used to describe someone who is employed to make coffee drinks or work behind the counter of a coffee shop.

Blend The act of combining coffees from different origins. Blending coffee beans is designed to produce a unique, signature taste.

Blonde Beans with a shorter roasting time; light-bodied and allowing for a more mellow flavor.

Body The weight or thickness of a coffee brew. This is the sensation of heaviness when one tastes coffee. Examples of body categories are light, medium, and full.

Bouquet The smell of the coffee grounds.

Breve Espresso made with cream.

Brew A drink made by boiling, steeping, or mixing various ingredients.

C Contract The C is the world benchmark market pricing for arabica coffee. Those in the coffee industry view the C Contract as a guide to the cost of business.

C.A.F.E. Coffee and Farmer Equity Practices, Starbucks coffee verification program.

Caffeine A bitter alkaloid found in coffee, tea, and various other plant parts. It stimulates the central nervous system, causing increased alertness, energy, and attention.

Cappuccino A beverage made from espresso, hot steamed milk, and frothed milk. The drink is typically made with one-third espresso, one-third steamed milk, and one-third frothed milk on top. The frothed milk is sometimes sprinkled with cinnamon or powdered chocolate. The drink (Italian for little Capuchin) gets its name from the Capuchin order of Franciscan friars, because the whipped cream rising to a point resembled a friar with his long, pointed brown hood, or *capuche*, pulled up.

Cherry The ripened fruit of the coffee tree. The plant actually resembles a tall bush or shrub. The fruits are referred to as coffee cherries and are bright red when ready to pick. Coffee beans are the pits of the coffee cherry. Most coffee cherries contain two beans, but occasionally (in roughly 5–10 percent of fruits) only one bean is produced by a cherry. This single bean is called a peaberry. Coffee cherries are hand-picked by farmers.

Clean A coffee that is free from flavor defects.

Coffee leaf rust A disease that has devastating consequences for coffee farms, presenting as an orange powdery rust on the coffee leaves.

Coffee Quality Institute (CQI) A nonprofit organization formed to improve the quality of coffee and the lives of the people who produce it.

Cooperative Also known as a co-op, a farm that is run in cooperation with others. Many small farms may work together in order to strengthen their economic power.

Cupping Tasting coffee; a procedure used by professional tasters to test a coffee's quality. Cupping allows one to compare coffee samples with each other.

Dark roast The darkest style of roasting coffee beans that produces a deep, rich, full-bodied cup of coffee.

Decaffeinated Having the caffeine removed; this may apply to coffee, tea, or other products. Decaffeinating coffee is achieved through a variety of decaffeination methods. For those affected negatively by caffeine, decaffeinated (or *decaf*) coffee is an alternative. Almost all brands of decaffeinated coffee still contain some trace levels of caffeine.

Espresso A strong, concentrated coffee made by forcing hot water through finely ground coffee beans under pressure. It is used as a main component for coffee drinks, such as Americanos, cappuccinos, and lattes.

Fair-trade coffee Coffee that has been purchased from farmers at a fair, above-market price intended to raise the living standards of small-scale coffee farmers.

Finish The taste that is left on the palate after the coffee is spat out or swallowed.

Flat White A coffee beverage made with espresso and a thin, or flat, layer of steamed milk on top.

Flavor A sensory evaluation of coffee after the merging of aroma, acidity, and body.

Fragrance The smell of coffee after the beans have been ground.

Grade The classification of green coffee by size and density of the beans.

Green beans The seeds contained within the coffee fruits that, when roasted and ground, yield coffee. Usually greenish in color, they can range from dull beige to light green, jade, or even blue-green.

Green coffee Raw coffee beans that have not been roasted.

Hard bean Coffee grown at relatively high altitudes—4,000–4,500 feet. Coffee grown above 4,500 feet is referred to as strictly hard bean. Beans grown at higher altitudes mature more slowly and are harder and denser than other beans, and thus more desirable.

Instant coffee Brewed coffee that is dehydrated to make it instantly soluble when mixed with hot water.

International Coffee Organization (ICO) The main intergovernmental organization for coffee, founded in London in 1963, in collaboration with the United Nations. The ICO is responsible for addressing the challenges of the global coffee sector through international cooperation. Members include forty-three exporting countries, along with six importing countries. These forty-nine member countries account for more than 98 percent of world coffee production and 67 percent of world coffee consumption.

Java An island of Indonesia that is a big producer of coffee and gave its name to a generic cup of coffee.

Joe Also *cup of joe*. A slang name for coffee, named after Admiral Josephus "Joe" Daniels, U.S. Chief of Naval Operations, who outlawed alcohol on board ships in 1914, and ordered coffee as the beverage of service.

Latte A coffee beverage made with espresso and topped with steamed milk. Often, the ratio is one-third espresso topped with two-thirds steamed milk.

Macchiato Generally speaking, the Italian term means marked. An espresso macchiato is espresso marked with a small amount of foamed milk.

Medium roast The roast level between light and dark, which produces a well-rounded and balanced cup of coffee.

Mocha A type of high-quality coffee bean from Arabia. This term also describes a beverage combining chocolate and a form of coffee, usually espresso.

National Coffee Association (NCA) The National Coffee Association USA was founded in 1911 and was the first trade association for the coffee industry in the United States. Its widely referenced *National Coffee Drinking Trends* study has monitored U.S. coffee consumption since 1950. The NCA has members from over 300 companies across the coffee industry and represents more than 1.6 million jobs in the United States alone.

Nose The sensation of vapors released by the brewed coffee in the mouth.

Organic coffee Produced without the use of synthetic pesticides, herbicides, or chemical fertilizers. To be *certified organic*, farmers must verify that they are using accepted organic practices and undergo soil testing. Certification can therefore be costly and accounts for the higher prices of many organic coffees.

Roast To brown green coffee beans by drying and exposing to heat; the process of transforming green coffee beans into roasted coffee. The darker the roast, the heavier the flavor.

Robusta A poorer quality of coffee and less expensive compared to the superior arabica. Robusta is usually used for lower-quality coffee blends and is utilized in jars of instant coffee and mass supermarket-grade blends. Arabica coffee is generally utilized in coffeehouses and specialty food and grocery stores. Robusta coffee has a high caffeine content, with nearly twice as much caffeine as arabica coffee. Robusta is a hardier coffee plant that is more resistant to weather conditions, has a greater crop yield, and requires less care than arabica. Its taste is harsh.

Shade grown Refers to coffee grown underneath a canopy, often formed by other trees. Contrast this with coffee grown in direct sunlight. Shade-grown coffee implies organic or other ecologically sensitive growing conditions.

Single-origin coffee Coffee from a specific growing region.

Soft bean Describes coffee grown at relatively low altitudes—below 4,000 feet. Coffee plants grown at lower altitudes mature more quickly and produce a lighter, more porous bean.

Specialty coffee Also referred to as gourmet or premium coffee. These coffees are made from superior beans grown in ideal climates. Specialty coffees tend to produce distinctive flavors, unique to the regions in which they were grown.

Specialty Coffee Association (SCA) The Specialty Coffee Association of America and the Specialty Association of Europe combined in 2017 to form the Specialty Coffee Association (SCA). The most influential and recognized authority on specialty coffee, the association involves members from baristas to producers. Offices are located in Santa Ana, California, and in Chelmsford, UK.

Ton A metric ton; the measurement used in coffee shipments.

Tryer A tool located on the drum roaster, used to capture a sample of coffee during the roasting process.

Whole-bean coffee Roasted coffee beans not yet ground.

Acronyms

CAP—Canada, Asia, Pacific

C.A.F.E.—Coffee and Farmer Equity (in Starbucks C.A.F.E. Practices)

CEO—Chief executive officer

CERT—Council of Education and Research on Toxics

CFO—Chief financial officer

CI—Conservation International

COLAP—Community Organizations Legal Assistance Project

COO—Chief operating officer

COVID-19—Coronavirus disease 2019

CQI—Coffee Quality Institute

CSR—Corporate social responsibility

EMEA—Europe, Middle East, Africa

EPS—Earnings per share

FAFSA—Free Application for Federal Student Aid

FY—Fiscal year

GAAP—Generally Accepted Accounting Principles

GDP—Gross domestic product

GIS—Geographic information systems

GS—Global select

ICBI—Indianapolis Community Building Institute

ICE—Intercontinental Exchange

ICO—International Coffee Organization

INHP—Indianapolis Neighborhood Housing Partnership

INRC—The Indianapolis Neighborhood Resource Center

IPO—Initial public offering

IWW—Industrial Workers of the World

IT—Information Technology

kg—Kilogram

LEED—Leadership in Energy and Environmental Design green building rating system

LGBTQ—Lesbian, gay, bisexual, transgender, queer or questioning

LISC—Local Initiatives Support Corporation

LK—Luckin Corporation common stock

MCANA—Marion County Alliance of Neighborhood Associations

NASDAQ—National Association Securities Dealers Automated Quotations

NBER—National Bureau of Economic Research

NCA—National Coffee Association

NLRB—National Labor Relations Board

OTC—Over the counter

P/E—Price-to-earnings ratio

PCF—Post-consumer recycled fiber

PR—Public relations

Q—Quarter

RTD—Ready to Drink

SBUX—Starbucks Corporation common stock

SCA—Specialty Coffee Association

SEC—Securities and Exchange Commission

SGA—Starbucks Global Academy

SIP—Stock Investment Plan

SWU—Starbucks Workers Union

TSP—Team Service Projects

TTM—Trailing twelve months

IDB—Inter-American Developmental Bank

UK—United Kingdom

USAID—U.S. Agency for International Development

USD—U.S. dollars

USDA—U.S. Department of Agriculture

UWCI—United Way of Central Indiana

VP—Vice president

Wi-Fi—Wireless fidelity

Directory of Resources

Starbucks-Related Websites

https://www.starbucks.com

Just like Starbucks coffee, Starbucks' online presence is exceptional. Fans of the company can spend hours perusing this website through a multitude of coffee, tea, and menu choices. Thinking about lunching at Starbucks but don't know what food options are available? Check out Starbucks Food and discover Smoked Turkey Protein Box with 24 grams of protein and only 360 calories. For those who might like to indulge, check out the Crispy Grilled Cheese Sandwich on sourdough bistro bread for 540 calories coupled with Iced Lemon Loaf Cake for dessert at 460 calories.

Having a busy day and want to skip the cash register at your local Starbucks? This website allows you to download the highly popular Mobile Order & Pay app. You can order on the app, walk in and, without waiting in line, ask a barista for your freshly made order at the pick-up area. Additionally, if you are lucky enough to be in a city where Uber Eats delivers Starbucks, you can download the Uber Eats app for quick delivery of your favorite beverage and treat.

Everything Starbucks, even employment opportunities, is just a click away. You can search for job openings with the company—retail, retail leadership, corporate, manufacturing and distribution—and apply directly on the website. If you just want to learn more about the Starbucks Corporation, About Us will route you to the company mission and a detailed company timeline, or take you to the investor relations page where you can get the financial lowdown. The Press Center is top-notch for anyone interested in company activity; you can check out current news and scan historical quick reads.

https://www.starbucksreserve.com/en-us

Starbucks Reserve™, the company's premium roast variety, can be experienced in one of three ways—option one, visit a Starbucks Reserve Roastery; option two, spend time at a Reserve Coffee Bar; or option three, locate Starbucks Reserve™ coffee at select Starbucks locations. This website will assist you in your coffee loving journey. All Starbucks Reserve Roastery facilities roast coffee beans on location and allow you to view as well as package and enjoy the specialty single-origin coffees like Kenya Barichu or Sun-Dried Brazil Vale Verde Estate.

Roastery locations include Seattle, Shanghai, Milan, New York, Tokyo, and Chicago, with additional locations planned. Photos on the website display the trendy, chic vibe for each locale. You can sip coffee in Seattle's library with more than 200 titles on coffee or stop by Green Bean Station in Shanghai, the initial stop for incoming burlap bags of green coffee beans before storage until roasting. The Starbucks Reserve Coffee Bars are high end and allow for a unique coffee experience, serving Starbucks Reserve™ along with a bit of education from baristas on coffee techniques and brewing processes.

Taking a trip to watch the Chicago Cubs? Be sure to visit the Wrigley Field Reserve Coffee Bar. Shopping spree at Macy's in New York? Relax on Macy's second floor at the Reserve Coffee Bar. Journeying to London to see Big Ben and Buckingham Palace? Rest your feet at Upper St. Martins Lane in London at the Reserve Coffee Bar. While you may not be traveling, we all have an opportunity to experience Starbucks Reserve coffee by using the map locations on the navigation menu. Find seasonal, limited-quantity Starbucks Reserve coffee at 1,500-plus Starbucks locations. Stop in for one of the limited-time high-end coffees. You can easily identify Reserve Roastery locations, Reserve Coffee Bars, and Starbucks Reserve™ coffee by the notable star and the R logo.

https://stories.starbucks.com

A new storytelling platform, Starbucks Stories became available to Starbucks devotees in early 2019. A compilation of videos, photos, written stories, and more combine to make this site the epitome of a Starbucks gallery. The navigation menu lists Coffee, Community, Social Impact, News, and the Press Center. Click Coffee to watch the film *HINGAKAWA: An Original Starbucks Productions Documentary* by director and producer Luanne Dietz. This riveting and impactful 18-minute film allows you to visit Hingakawa, a coffee co-op run by women who find strength and support in one another following the Rwandan genocide.

Scroll through Community and you will see *New Tokyo Roastery: top 10 things to know* by Kylie Grader. Check out #7 to learn this fully operational roastery roasts almost 750 tons of coffee per year for the Japanese market. Under Social Impact, *Say hello to the lid that will replace a billion straws a year* by Jennifer Warnick gives a glimpse of and discussion on the new lightweight strawless cold drink lid which will be a force behind eliminating plastic straws worldwide by 2020.

News covers countless articles including *Starbucks 2019 Annual Meeting* by Joshua Trujillo. Check out photos of the March 20, 2019 event in downtown Seattle at the WaMu Theater. A particularly eventful annual meeting, guests could rake coffee in a simulated drying patio and sample various Starbucks beverages at thirteen serving stations. Download a Company Profile Fact Sheet from the Press Center if you enjoy historical trivia. Did you know Starbucks went public on June 26, 1992, at a price of $17 per share and closed on the first day of trading at $21.50 per share? Keep reading the stories for a Starbucks education.

https://ideas.starbucks.com

My Starbucks Idea was started in 2008 by Howard Schulz as a community website for customers to provide feedback and suggestions for the company. While the original website was a community involvement page where customers could vote on ideas presented, the current idea site is streamlined, but still community minded. The page is simple and down to business. The headline: "What's Your Idea? Revolutionary or simple—we want to hear it." This is not a token gesture; Starbucks really means it. Partners review each idea submitted. Through the years such glorious gems as cake pops and splash sticks developed from community suggestions. You will be prompted to summarize your suggestion and categorize its theme. Which of the following themes fits your proposal—a new idea or suggestion; an improvement to an existing; a request to bring back a product; or other? Click and write to your heart's content, as long as you keep your idea to 500 words or less. Be a Starbucks insider or at least feel like one. When you are done composing and submitting, Starbucks responds, "Thank you for sharing your idea with us."

Coffee-Related Websites

https://sca.coffee

The Specialty Coffee Association (SCA) is a nonprofit, membership-based organization that represents thousands of specialty coffee professionals.

Specialty coffee has a richer, more balanced flavor than commercial coffee, and the SCA is committed to collaborating with members so the specialty coffee industry can flourish. With affiliates representing more than forty countries, SCA is the world's largest coffee trade association with offices in Santa Ana, California, and Chelmsford, Essex. Along with company memberships the SCA offers a variety of options for coffee career types—barista, roaster, technician—and even a professional membership, if you love coffee but don't fall into one of the select categories. Scan the membership category and see all the goodies that come along with joining this esteemed organization. A barista membership permits one to also join either the prestigious Barista Guild of America or the Barista Guild of Europe. Keep on clicking to find a host of other opportunities that enrollment provides.

You don't need a membership to learn all about specialty coffee on this website. Investigate *A Botanists' Guide to Specialty Coffee Facts and Figures* to become a self-taught expert on gourmet coffee. Did you know that arabica constitutes approximately 70 percent of the world's coffee production and makes up most of the world's specialty market? Of all the *Coffea* species, only arabica is self-pollinating, plus arabica has a lower caffeine count than canephora (typically known as robusta). Your specialty coffee education continues by reading such intriguing articles as *Baristas: Coffee Culture's Ambassadors* by Elizabeth Doerr, and *Why the Specialty Coffee Industry Should Strive for Inclusive Design* by Hoby Wedler and Trey Malone in SCA's *25 Magazine*.

https://www.ico.org

The International Coffee Organization (ICO) was founded in London in 1963 and is the main intergovernmental body of forty-three coffee-exporting and six coffee-importing member countries. Global coffee meetings, events, and conferences are all here to see with just a click or two. If you want trade statistics or coffee prices in select countries, you need not look any further. FYI: World production of exporting countries for the coffee year 2017–2018 was at 163.51 million bags, with Brazil, the world's largest producer of coffee, accounting for 57.4 million bags.

If you would like to pretend you are player in the global coffee sector, or you are simply intrigued by international business, grab a seat at the World Coffee Conference. Every four to six years, the ICO holds a sophisticated conference, with the first four held in England (2001), Brazil (2005), Guatemala (2010), and Ethiopia (2016). Watch, read, and delve into the activities and opinions of the global movers and shakers.

If you are in a celebratory mood, check out International Coffee Day, officially October 1, and recognized on or around that date, for events around the globe. It may be called Coffee Day or National Coffee Day in your country, but it signifies an international celebration of the beloved drink. If you are into heavy reading, access the most recent ICO's annual review for data, analysis, and coffee information to appreciate the significant economic impact of coffee. You might also pick up an educational fact, like hemileia vasatrix, an orange powdery fungus, is commonly referred to as coffee leaf rust and is a devastating disease for coffee growers. To be sure, if it is coffee related around the globe, you can probably find your answer on this highly detailed website.

https://www.ncausa.org

The National Coffee Association (NCA) USA, founded in 1911 and based in New York, was the first trade association for the U.S. coffee industry. The NCA proudly represents the industry from crop to cup. If you are in the business, this is your go-to website, with market research, economic impact studies, and industry sources. It is overflowing with practical tips for the home brewer too. You can spend hours reading the consumer-friendly About Coffee sections. At your fingertips: *What Is Coffee, History of Coffee, 10 Steps from Seed to the Cup, How to Store Coffee, How to Brew Coffee, Coffee Roast Guide*, and *Coffee around the World*. You will be an industry professional after absorbing this coffee curriculum.

A good cup of coffee starts with the bean choice. Kona coffee from the big island in Hawaii will produce a delicious rich, aromatic cup of medium body coffee. Kenyan coffee is a fruity acidy bean, full bodied with a rich fragrance. Perhaps you prefer a coffee with light acidity and mild body? Vietnam coffee may be your pick. The country is quickly emerging as one of the world's heavy hitters, producing mostly robusta, a milder choice. Prepared coffee begins to lose its optimal taste shortly after the brewing process, so drink up and enjoy.

https://coffeecenter.ucdavis.edu

The Coffee Center at University of California, Davis, was founded in 2013 to provide educational opportunities along with engaging in vital coffee research. UC Davis is already a world leader in beer and wine brewing research and, as you can see from the website, Coffee Center is moving forward with gusto. Check out the thirty-five professors at UC Davis with expertise in coffee research, along with the 1,200-square-foot undergraduate coffee lab dedicated to coffee science. Click on the

Undergraduate Coffee Lab tab and you will find a host of companies, including Starbucks, who have donated equipment or coffee beans to the research lab. Scroll through Education and you will get the drift that Coffee Center has some lofty goals, including the one-of-a-kind master's degree in Coffee Science that UC Davis is in the process of creating. Voted the most popular general education course on campus, The Design of Coffee: An Engineering Approach treats students to a nonmathematical approach to chemical engineering via the roasting and brewing of coffee. Coffee experiments demonstrate engineering principles, with students ultimately competing to make the tastiest coffee brew utilizing the least amount of energy. Even if you aren't a student at UC Davis, you can visit the Coffee Center vicariously by watching the caffeine-charged UC Davis Coffee Center video.

Podcasts

Oprah's Super Soul Conversations

Oprah Winfrey encourages listeners to "awaken, discover, and connect to the deeper meaning" of the world around them. You will certainly be more enlightened and inspired after listening to Oprah's selection of interviews with best-selling authors, spiritual leaders, health and wellness experts, and business titans. Enjoy the multitude of podcasts Oprah has made available and be sure you don't miss the episode from September 13, 2017, entitled *Howard Schultz: Pouring Your Heart into Your Business*. A blunt conversation with the now Chairman Emeritus of Starbucks, Schultz takes you back to his childhood growing up in the projects, a challenging time for Schultz and his family, but a motivator that drew him to achieve super success. If you don't have time to read Schultz's 2011 *Onward* or 2019 *From the Ground Up*, a half-hour of podcasting will provide a glimpse of the man. Revealed is his motivation to bring comprehensive health care to all Starbucks employees, including part-timers. You will get to know the person and share his enthusiasm and desire. A favorite quote from the interview, Schultz referenced "luck is the residue of design." Discussions focus on the slowdown during the recession with Starbucks' growth and success covering up mistakes. Learn how the coffee magnate returned the company to its glory days following the recession. Oprah concludes by asking Schultz to fill in the blank: "My job is _____." Schultz quickly responds, "To serve others."

Filter Stories

Creator of Filter Stories, expressive James Harper, will take you through a variety of investigative stories all related to the coffee industry. The podcast started in 2018 and hit with gusto to rave reviews, revealing the "untold stories hidden in your cup of coffee." James knows his coffee, having worked as an international wholesale manager for The Barn and business development manager for Grinders Coffee. Lose yourself in the intriguing sound mix which accompanies the stories. Here is just a taste of the A+ journalism.

Venezuela features the Bermejo brothers who struggle to buy a coffee shop in Caracas while the country begins its economic downfall. Struggles and strategies abound for older brother Eduardo and younger brother Andres. You will be taken on a journey with ultimately a positive outcome and the opening of a coffee company in Panama. Does the last name sound familiar to coffee lovers? Perhaps, because Eduardo was the 2017 Panama Barista Champion.

If you are interested in coffee and coffee people, check out *Stateless*, where you will meet Mikhail, a 39-year-old specialty coffee barista stranded on the island of Samoa. Still stateless, you will follow Mikhail's exhaustive journey to return to the United States. Spoiler alert—Mikhail spends every day on his computer at McDonald's, contacting lawyers, friends, officials, or anyone who might help him get off the island.

Tito follows a coffee farmer from Panama who opted to buy a coffee farm in lieu of pursuing his education. Tito, a professed coffee lover, worked through high school in the 1980s, saving $20,000 to buy a coffee farm. His parents wanted him to invest his money in education to become an engineer and have an easier life. He quickly finds the coffee farming life hard as he discovers the soil is damaged from use as a cattle farm. It is quite a voyage for Tito to become a highly prized coffee roaster.

The Coffee Podcast

Coffee and people, hosted by cofounder Jesse Hartman, is the theme of The Coffee Podcast, which has been running since 2015. Jesse holds fascinating conversations with people around the world in the coffee industry. A former barista and manager in various coffee ventures, his podcast is often directed to the individuals involved in making the coffee. Episodes 1 through 110 were released weekly, with current episodes being released in a series, every four months. Here are a few favorites.

Episode 97, *Understanding the Coffee Market,* provides financial insight into pricing for the volatile coffee market. For 34 minutes you will listen to Judy Ganes, a seasoned soft commodities specialist, addressing questions surrounding pricing in the coffee market. Commodity trading manages the volatility of coffee price shifts from supply and demand conditions. Did you know the market has a gravitational pull from $1.20 to $1.40 a pound? Judy also has practical wisdom to share, noting coffee is such a social beverage and the fabric of so many communities. When coffee prices are depressed, communities and economies suffer, resulting in entire social fallout.

Episode 124, *Coffee Myths: Arabica vs. Robusta (pt. 1),* addresses the age-old coffee controversy of which is better, arabica or robusta coffee? Hanna Neuschwander, Communications Director of World Coffee Research, gleefully discusses the pros and cons of each variety. If you have 43 minutes and want to familiarize yourself with the two main varieties of coffee, arabica and robusta, lend an ear. Jesse and Hanna quickly concede that arabica is thought of as the premier coffee, the winner for taste. Hanna confirms that robusta has some strengths for farmers, including it being more adaptable to a wider range of environments, can be grown at lower altitudes, and is more tolerant to heat. Yes, this coffee talker alludes there is even a possibility of a high-quality robusta.

Episode 131, *Coffee Myths: What Is Direct Trade REALLY?* touches on a hot topic in the industry. Direct trade is a phrase tossed around in the specialty coffee sector, but has many different interpretations. Henry Wilson, CEO of *The Perfect Daily Grind,* a digital coffee publication, talks for 30 minutes on this unregulated term. Direct trade is the connection between the coffee roasters and the producers. Henry says this phrase has become antiquated, used, and abused. Looking at the various actors along the coffee chain, if they add value, they are important and necessary, according to Henry. Should consumers look for a direct trade label on a bag? Tune in to listen to Wilson's explanation and recommendation.

Unpacking Coffee

This mesmerizing podcast, video included, will keep you coming back for more. Hosted by Ray and Kandace Brigleb of Needmore Productions, the name "Unpacking Coffee" says it all. Simply explained, in each podcast episode the duo unpacks a specialty roast coffee and explores. You will be privy to such stories as the history of the companies, mission and philosophies, design templates, and sources of coffee. Let's explore a sampling of their coffee chats so you get the flavor.

You will meet the founder and owner of Atlanta's Radio Roasters, Chip Gradbow, in a quick 7 minutes from Episode 24: *Radio Roasters*. Chip founded Radio Roasters in 2013 after a career working at NPR and CNN. The surprise is there is no retail establishment; subscription services are encouraged from this micro-roastery. Chips suggests consumers replenish their stock every two or three weeks in order to keep the coffee fresh and this enables coffee drinkers to try something new. The more coffee you order, the more bags you can explore. Chip has created a super trendy radio vibe on each bag—white ink on a craft bag with stamps galore.

Episode 61: *Equator* features cofounder and CEO Helen Russell from Equator Coffees and Teas, of San Rafael, California. In 9 minutes you will pick up fascinating facts such as the name Equator was chosen because the coffee and tea are grown along the equator, and the Bengal tiger on the bold red package is because the tiger is of vital concern to the owners (her co-owner is Brooke McDonnell). Concerned about the Bengal tigers because of poaching, the company even pays a social premium to coffee purchased in Sumatra with the premium going to the Sumatran Tiger Trust. This is a company that is socially minded. Helen talks with pride about buying a coffee farm in Panama and building worker housing for the people that work the land.

If you have 12 minutes and want to take a quick trip to Nashville, check out Episode 64: *Barista Parlor*. Managing Director Christopher Ayers proudly chats his way through the history of the retail company that roasts their own coffee, noting the company combines art and commerce. The packaging is unique because the coffee is encased in a bag, then placed in the box. The coffee explored during this episode—Dare-Devil, a blend coffee—features an old-fashioned dare devil rider on the front of the box, with creative and imaginative art.

Bibliography

About Starbucks Union. Starbucks Workers Union. Available at www.starbuck sunion.org (accessed January 17, 2009).

Adamy, J. "Starbucks Tests $1 Cup of Coffee, Free Refills." *Wall Street Journal*, January 23, 2008. Available at www.online.wsj.com (accessed January 2, 2009).

Allison, M. "As Stores Close Starbucks Buys a Jet." *Seattle Times*, January 8, 2009. Available at www.seattletimes.nwsource.com (accessed March 10, 2009).

Allison, M. "Starbucks Puts Third Corporate Jet Up for Sale." *Seattle Times*, March 6, 2009. Available at www.seattletimes.nwsource.com (accessed March 10, 2009).

Allison, M. "Starbucks Sued Over Unchecked Ambition." *Seattle Times*, September 26, 2006. Available at www.seattletimes.nwsource.com (accessed January 7, 2009).

Allison, M. "Starbucks Trying to Sell Its New Jet." *Seattle Times*, January 28, 2009. Available at www.seattletimes.nwsource.com (accessed March 10, 2009).

Anderson, R. "Starbucks Antitrust Lawsuit Settled." *Daily Weekly*, May 30, 2008. Available at www.blogs.seattleweekly.com/dailyweekly/ (accessed January 7, 2009).

Andrejczak, M. "Starbucks CEO Seeks to Dispel 'Excess' Myth." *MarketWatch*, March 18, 2009. Available at www.marketwatch.com (accessed April 10, 2009).

Behar, H., and J. Goldstein. *It's Not about the Coffee: Leadership Principles from a Life at Starbucks*. New York: Penguin Group, 2007.

Boeing: Higher, Faster, Farther: 1970–1996. Boeing. Available at www.boeing.com (accessed September 7, 2008).

"BofA to Sell 3 Corporate Jets, Helicopter." Associated Press Charlotte (AP) *News & Record*, February 4, 2009. Available at www.news-record.com (accessed March 13, 2009).

Business Cycle Dating Committee, National Bureau of Economic Research. *Determination of the December 2007 Peak in Economic Activity*. December 11, 2008. Available at www.nber.org (accessed January 20, 2009).

Capuchin Franciscan Frequently Asked Questions. The Capuchin Franciscans. Available at www.beafriar.com (accessed January 12, 3009).

Clark, T. *A Double Tall Tale of Caffeine, Commerce, and Culture*. New York: Little, Brown and Company, 2007.

Coffee. National Geographic, 1999. Available at www.nationalgeographic.com (accessed August 15, 2008).

Dunkin Brand Group Inc. Form 10-K, filed February 24, 2020. United States Securities and Exchange Commission, Washington, DC.

EthosWater: Helping Children Get Clean Water. EthosWater, c/o Starbucks Coffee Company. Available at www.ethoswater.com (accessed January 15, 2009).

Fact Sheet: Starbucks Partners and Unions. Starbucks Coffee Company, August 8, 2006. Available at www.starbucks.com (accessed January 17, 2009).

Fellner, K. *Wrestling with Starbucks: Conscience, Capital, and Cappuccino*. New Brunswick, NJ: Rutgers University Press, 2008.

Herbst, M. "Starbucks' Union Blues." *Business Week*, December 31, 2008. Available at www.businessweek.com (accessed January 17, 2009).

Hewitt, R., Jr. *Coffee: Its History, Cultivation, and Uses*. New York: D. Appleton and Company, 1872. rpt. University of Michigan University Library.

History of Coffee. Starbucks Coffee Company, 2008. Available at www.starbucks.com (accessed August 15, 2008).

Hubbard, R. G., and A. P. O'Brien. *Microeconomics*, 2nd edition. Upper Saddle River, NJ: Pearson Prentice Hall, 2008.

James, A. "6,700 Starbucks Jobs at Risk." *Seattle Post-Intelligencer*, January 29, 2009. Available at www.seattlepi.com (accessed March 1, 2009).

James, A. "Starbucks Won't Slug It Out in Ad Wars." *Seattle Post-Intelligencer*, December 10, 2008. Available at www.seattlepi.com (accessed January 4, 2009).

Logren, S. "Coffee-Based Log Burns Cleaner-But No Starbucks Smell." *National Geographic News*, October 25, 2004. Available at www.news.nationalgeographic.com/news (accessed June 12, 2009).

McDonald's Corporation Form 10-K, filed February 26, 2020. United States Securities and Exchange Commission, Washington, DC.

Michelli, J. *The Starbucks Experience: 5 Principles for Turning Ordinary into Extraordinary*. New York: McGraw-Hill, 2007.

Moore, J. *Tribal Knowledge: Business Wisdom Brewed from the Grounds of Starbucks Corporate Culture*. Chicago: Kaplan Publishing, 2006.

Mulady, K. "Retail Notebook: As Starbucks Marks 30th Year, a Look Back at Beginning." *Seattle Post-Intelligencer*, September 8, 2001. Available at www.seattlepi.com (accessed August 23, 2008).

News Release. "Howard Schultz Transformation Agenda Communication #3." Starbucks Coffee Company, January 30, 2008. Available at www.starbucks.com (accessed January 1, 2009).

News Release. "Inspire Brands, Inc. ("Inspire") today announced the completion of its $11.3 billion acquisition of Dunkin' Brands Group, Inc. ("Dunkin' Brands")."

Inspire Brands, Inc., December 15, 2020. Available at www.inspirebrands.com (accessed January 23, 2021).

News Release. "Starbucks Appoints Olden Lee as Interim Executive Vice President, Partner Resources." Starbucks Coffee Company, April 6, 2009. Available at www.news.starbucks.com (accessed April 9, 2009).

News Release. "Starbucks Details Strategy for Profitable Growth." Starbucks Coffee Company, March 18, 2009. Available at www.news.starbucks.com (accessed April 10, 2009).

News Release. "Starbucks Reports First Quarter Fiscal 2009 Results." Starbucks Coffee Company, January 28, 2009. Available at www.starbucks.com (accessed March 1, 2009).

News Release. "Starbucks Reports Fourth Quarter and Fiscal 2008 Results." Starbucks Coffee Company, November 10, 2008. Available at www.starbucks.com (accessed December 27, 2008).

News Release. "Starbucks Unveils New Strategic Initiatives to Transform and Innovate the Customer Experience." Starbucks Coffee Company, March 19, 2008. Available at www.starbucks.com (accessed December 10, 2008; February 16, 2009).

News Release. "Statement from Luckin Coffee." Luckin Coffee, January 7, 2021. Available at www.luckin.com (accessed January 23, 2001).

News Release. "Winner in the Battle of the Brews: Dunkin' Donuts Beat Starbucks in Independent Nationwide Taste Test." Dunkin' Donuts, October 30, 2008. Available at www.dunkindonuts.com (accessed January 3, 2009).

New York Board of Trade. *Coffee: Futures and Options*. New York: New York Board of Trade, 2004.

"People of the Year 95: Gerald Baldwin, Peet's Coffee & Tea." *Tea & Coffee Trade Journal*, December 1, 1995. Available at www.allbusiness.com (accessed September 8, 2008).

Ramsland, K. *The Starbucks Shooter*. TruTV, Turner Broadcasting System, Inc. Available at www.trutv.com (accessed December 30, 2008).

Ross, B., and C. Herman. "GM, Ford Will Sell Corporate Jet Fleet." *ABC News*, December 2, 2008. Available at www.abcnewsgo.com (accessed March 13, 2009).

Schiller, B. R. *The Micro Economy Today*, 11th edition. New York: McGraw-Hill Irwin, 2008.

Schultz, H., and D. Jones Yang. *Pour Your Heart into It: How Starbucks Built a Company One Cup at a Time*. New York: Hyperion, 1997.

Simmons, J. *My Sister's a Barista: How They Made Starbucks a Home Away from Home*. London: Cyan Books, 2005.

Specialty Coffee Association of America Fact Sheet: Specialty Coffee Facts. Specialty Coffee Association of America. Available at www.scaa.org (accessed January 8, 2009).

Specialty Coffee Association of America Fact Sheet: Specialty Coffee Retail in the U.S.A. 2006. Specialty Coffee Association of America. Available at www.scaa.org (accessed January 8, 2009).

Starbucks 2018 Annual Report. Securities and Exchange Commission, September 30, 2018. Available at https://investor.starbucks.com/ (accessed August 9, 2019).

Starbucks 2019 Annual Report. Securities and Exchange Commission, September 30, 2019. Available at https://investor.starbucks.com/ (accessed July 25, 2020).

Starbucks Coffee Company 02-CA-37548. The National Labor Relations Board Division of Judges New York Branch Office. Mindy E. Landow; December 19, 2008.

Starbucks Corporation Definitive Proxy Statement, January 22, 2021. United States Securities and Exchange Commission, Washington, DC.

Starbucks Corporation Form 8-K, filed February 9, 2009. United States Securities and Exchange Commission, Washington, DC.

Starbucks Corporation Form 8-K, filed March 5, 2020. United States Securities and Exchange Commission, Washington, DC.

Starbucks Corporation Form 10-K, filed November 24, 2008. United States Securities and Exchange Commission, Washington, DC.

Starbucks Corporation Form 10-K, filed February 4, 2009. United States Securities and Exchange Commission, Washington, DC.

Starbucks Corporation Form 10-K, filed November 12, 2020. United States Securities and Exchange Commission, Washington, DC.

"Starbucks Corp. SBUX Investor Day." Starbucks Coffee Company, December 9, 2020. Available at https://investor.starbucks.com/ (accessed January 24, 2021).

"Starbucks Corp. SBUX Q2 2019 Earnings Call." Starbucks Coffee Company, April 25, 2019. Available at https://investor.starbucks.com/ (accessed August 9, 2019).

"Starbucks Corp. SBUX Q3 Earnings Call." Starbucks Coffee Company, July 25, 2019. Available at https://investor.starbucks.com/ (accessed August 9, 2019).

"Starbucks Global Impact Report 2019." Starbucks Coffee Company, Starbucks Coffee Company, 2020. Available at https://globalassets.starbucks.com/ (accessed August 25, 2020).

Starbucks Investor Relations. "Starbucks Corp. Q4 2018 Earnings Call." Starbucks Coffee Company, Corrected Transcript November 1, 2018. Available at https://investor.starbucks.com (accessed December 16, 2019).

Starbucks Investor Relations. "Starbucks Corp. Q4 2019 Earnings Call." Starbucks Coffee Company, Corrected Transcript October 30, 2019. Available at https://investor.starbucks.com/ (accessed December 16, 2019).

Starbucks Investor Relations. "Starbucks Corp. Q2 2020 Earnings Call." Starbucks Coffee Company, Corrected Transcript April 28, 2020. Available at https://investor.starbucks.com/ (accessed July 25, 2020).

Starbucks Investor Relations. "Starbucks Corp. (SBUX) Annual General Meeting." Starbucks Coffee Company, Corrected Transcript March 18, 2020. Available at https://investor.starbucks.com (accessed July 28, 2020).

Starbucks Stories. "22 Million Coffee Trees from Starbucks 'One Tree for Every Bag.'" Starbucks Coffee Company, December 2, 2016. Available at https://starbucks.com (accessed August 25, 2020).

Starbucks Stories. "C.A.F.E. Practices: Starbucks Approach to Ethically Sourcing Coffee." Starbucks Coffee Company, February 28, 2020. Available at https://starbucks.com (accessed August 27, 2020).

Starbucks Stories. "Fact Sheet: Four Fundamentals of Brewing." Starbucks Coffee Company, April 2012. Available at https://starbucks.com (accessed August 27, 2020).

Starbucks Stories. "Farmer Support Centers Help Ensure Coffee's Future Farm by Farm." Starbucks Coffee Company, September 13, 2019. Available at https://starbucks.com (accessed August 20, 2020).

Starbucks Stories. "New Era of Music Debuts at Starbucks with Spotify." Starbucks Coffee Company, January 19, 2016. Available at https://starbucks.com (accessed December 17, 2019).

Starbucks Stories. "Offering to Serve: Starbucks Joins Effort to Help Speed Covid-19 Vaccination Delivery." Starbucks Coffee Company, January 17, 2021. Available at https://starbucks.com (accessed January 24, 2021).

Starbucks Stories. "Starbucks and USAID Empower Thousands of Columbian Coffee Farmers." Starbucks Coffee Company, March 20, 2017. Available at https://starbucks.com (accessed August 26, 2020).

Starbucks Stories. "Starbucks Coffee Expert Shares Secrets for Brewing Coffee at Home." Starbucks Coffee Company, April 25, 2015. Available at https://starbucks.com (accessed August 28, 2020).

Starbucks Stories. "Starbucks Foundation Supporting Community Response and Resilience during COVID-19." Starbucks Coffee Company, May 28, 2020. Available at https://starbucks.com (accessed July 28, 2020).

Starbucks Stories. "Starbucks Hacienda Alsacia." Starbucks Coffee Channel, April 25, 2017. Available at https://starbucks.com (accessed August 23, 2020).

Starbucks Stories. "Starbucks Invests in the Next Generation of Columbian Coffee Farmers." Starbucks Coffee Company, July 10, 2017. Available at https://starbucks.com (accessed August 26, 2020).

Starbucks Stories. "The Holiday Season Has Arrived at Starbucks." Starbucks Coffee Company, November 5, 2020. Available at https://starbucks.com (accessed January 22, 2021).

"Store Wars: Cappuccino Kings." *BBC News,* June 9, 2004. Available at www.news.bbc.co.uk (accessed January 10, 2009).

The Story of Coffee. International Coffee Organization. Available at www.ico.org (accessed August 14, 2008).

Sullivan, P. "Alfred Peet; Put Buzz in Gourmet Coffee." *Washington Post,* September 1, 2007. Available at www.washingtonpost.com (accessed January 1, 2009).

Toops, D. "Starbuck's David Olsen: Awakening a Passion for Coffee." *Food Processing,* August 1, 1996. Available at www.allbusiness.com (accessed October 10, 2008).

Wild, A. *Coffee: A Dark History*. New York: W.W. Norton & Company, Inc., 2004.

Williams, D. "Boston Tea Party." *The Encyclopedia Americana*, International edition. Danbury, CT: Grolier Incorporated, 2004.

Personal Interviews

Lingle, Ted (executive director, Coffee Quality Institute), interview by author, December 11, 2019.

Manfredi, Chris (president, Hawaii Coffee Association), interview by author, February 5, 2020.

Rubio, Vicki (program director, Public Allies), interview by author, July 10, 2019.

Spokesperson for ICE Futures U.S., interview by author, October 31, 2008.

Taylor, Anne-Marie (executive director, Indianapolis Neighborhood Resource Center), interview by author, July 10, 2019.

Index

About the Author

Marie A. Bussing holds a doctorate in economics and is Assistant Professor Emerita of Economics at the University of Southern Indiana. Bussing has 30 years of teaching experience in the fields of macroeconomics, microeconomics, and money and banking. In addition to the first edition, *Starbucks: Corporations That Changed the World*, she has numerous books to her credit including *Influential Economists*, *Profit from the Evening News*, *Money for Minors*, and *Deficit: Why Should I Care?*